C O N T E N T S

CHAPTER THREE: Perception: What You See Is What You Get

CHAPTER FOUR: Emotions: Feeling, Thinking, and Communicating

CHAPTER FIVE: Language: Barrier and Bridge

CHAPTER SIX: Nonverbal Communication: Messages Beyond Words

CHAPTER SEVEN: Listening: More Than Meets the Ear

CHAPTER EIGHT: Communication and Relational Dynamics

CHAPTER NINE: Interpersonal Communication in Close Relationships

CHAPTER TEN: Improving Communication Climates

CHAPTER ELEVEN: Managing Interpersonal Conflicts

CHAPTER ONE

A First Look at Interpersonal Communication

OUTLINE

Use this outline to take notes as you read the chapter in the text and/or as your instructor lectures in class.

I. **WHY WE COMMUNICATE**
   A. **Physical Needs**
   B. **Identity Needs**
   C. **Social Needs**
      1. Pleasure
      2. Affection
      3. Companionship
      4. Escape
      5. Relaxation
      6. Control
   D. **Practical Goals**
      1. Instrumental goals
         a. Influence other's behavior
         b. Career success
      2. Maslow's basic needs
         a. Physical
         b. Safety
         c. Social
         d. Self-esteem
         e. Self-actualization

II. **THE PROCESS OF COMMUNICATION**

A. **A Linear View**
   1. Sender
   2. Encodes
   3. Message
   4. Channel
   5. Receiver
   6. Decodes
   7. Noise
B. **A Transactional View**
   1. Communicator is simultaneously sender and receiver
   2. Environments
      a. Physical
      b. Cultural
      c. Experiential
   3. Noise
      a. External
      b. Physiological
      c. Psychological
   4. Transactional communication is done with others simultaneously
C. **Defining Interpersonal communication**
D. **Interpersonal and Impersonal Communication**
E. **Quantitative approach to Interpersonal Communication**
   1. Dyad
   2. Impersonal communication
F. **Qualitative Approach**
   1. uniqueness
   2. irreplaceability
   3. interdependence
   4. disclosure
   5. intrinsic rewards

III. **COMMUNICATION PRINCIPLES AND MISCONCEPTIONS**
   A. **Communication Principles**
      1. Communication can be

2

intentional or unintentional

    2. It's impossible not to communicate

    3. Communication is unrepeatable

    4. Communication is irreversible

    5. Communication has a content and a relational dimension.

B. Communication Misconceptions

    1. More communication is not always better

    2. Meanings are not in words

    3. Successful communication doesn't always involve shared understanding

    4. Communication will not solve all problems

IV. SOCIAL MEDIA AND INTERPERSONAL COMMUNICATION

    A. Benefits of Social Media

      1. Low friction opportunities to create, enhance, and rediscover social ties

      2. Maintaining and rekindling relationships

      3. Minimizes perception differences

      4. Increase in "real life" social interaction

    B. Challenges of Social Media

      1. Leaner messages

        a. richness

        b. leanness

      2. Disinhibition

        a. volunteering of personal information

        b. highly expressive directness

      3. Permanence

3

V. WHAT MAKES AN EFFECTIVE COMMUNICATOR?

A. **Communication Competence Defined**
1. There is no ideal way to communicate
2. Competence is situational
3. Competence is relational
4. Competence can be learned

B. **Characteristics of Competent Communicators**
1. Wide range of behaviors
2. Ability to choose most appropriate behavior
   a. context
   b. goal
   c. knowledge of the other person
3. Skill at performing behaviors
   a. Beginning awareness
   b. Awkwardness
   c. Skillfulness
   d. Integration
4. Cognitive complexity
5. Empathy
6. Self-monitoring
7. Commitment
   a. Commitment to the other person
   b. Commitment to the message

C. **Competence in Intercultural Communication**
1. Co-cultures
2. Learn specific cultural rules
3. Motivation
4. Tolerance for ambiguity
5. Open-mindedness
6. Knowledge and skill

4

a. passive observation
b. active strategies
c. self-disclosure
D. Competence in Social Media
  1. Think before you post
  2. Be considerate
    a. respect others' need for undivided attention
    b. keep your tone civil
    c. don't intrude on bystanders
	_____
	
	_____
	
	_____
	
	_____
	
	_____

KEY TERMS

channel

co-culture

cognitive complexity

communication

communication competence

content dimension

decode

disinhibition

dyad

encode

environment

impersonal communication

instrumental goals

interpersonal

communication

linear communication model

message

noise

receiver

ACTIVITIES

1.1 COMMUNICATION SKILLS INVENTORY

LEARNING OBJECTIVES

- Assess the needs (physical, identity, social, and practical) that communicators are attempting to satisfy in a given situation or relationship.
- Diagnose the effectiveness of various communication channels in a specific situation.

INSTRUCTIONS

1. Below you will find several communication-related situations. As you read each item, imagine yourself in that situation.
2. For each instance, answer the following question: *How satisfied am I with the way I would communicate in this situation and ones like it?* You can express your answers by placing one of the following numbers in the space by each item:

5 = Completely satisfied with my probable action
4 = Generally, though not totally, satisfied with my probable action
3 = About equally satisfied and dissatisfied with my probable action
2 = Generally, though not totally, dissatisfied with my probable action
1 = Totally dissatisfied with my probable action

_____ 1. A new acquaintance has just shared some personal experiences with you that make you think you'd like to develop a closer relationship. You have experienced the same things and are now deciding whether to reveal these personal experiences.

_____ 2. You've become involved in a political discussion with someone whose views are the complete opposite of yours. The other person asks, "Can't you at least understand why I feel as I do?"

_____ 3. You are considered a responsible adult by virtually everyone except one relative who still wants to help you make all your decisions. You value your relationship with this person, but you want to be seen as more independent.

_____ 4. In a mood of self-improvement a friend asks you to describe the one or two ways you think he or she could behave better. You're willing to do so, but need to express yourself in a clear and helpful way.

_____ 5. A close companion tells you that you've been behaving "differently" lately and asks if you know what he or she means.

6

_____ 6. You've grown to appreciate a new friend a great deal lately, and you want to express your feelings to this friend.

_____ 7. An amateur writer you know has just shown you his or her latest batch of poems and asked your opinion of them. You don't think they are very good. It's time for your reply.

_____ 8. You've found certain behaviors of an important person in your life have become more and more bothersome to you. It's getting harder to keep your feelings to yourself.

_____ 9. You're invited to a party at which everyone except the host will be a stranger to you. Upon hearing about this, a friend says, "Gee, if I were going I'd feel like an outsider. They probably won't have much to do with you." How do you feel?

_____ 10. A friend comes to you feeling very upset about a recent incident and asks for advice. You suspect that there is more to the problem than just this one incident. You really want to help the friend.

_____ 11. You find yourself defending the behavior of a friend against the criticisms of a third person. The critic accuses you of seeing only what you want to see and ignoring the rest.

_____ 12. A boss or instructor asks you to explain a recent assignment to a companion who has been absent. You are cautioned to explain the work clearly so there will be no misunderstandings.

_____ 13. You ask an acquaintance for help with a problem. She says yes, but the way the message is expressed leaves you thinking she'd rather not. You do need the help, but only if it's sincerely offered.

_____ 14. A roommate always seems to be too busy to do the dishes when it's his or her turn, and you've wound up doing them most of the time. You resent the unequal sharing of responsibility and want to do something about it.

_____ 15. A new acquaintance has become quite interested in getting to know you better, but you feel no interest yourself. You've heard that this person is extremely sensitive and insecure.

By totaling your score for all of the items you can get an idea of how satisfied you are with your overall ability to communicate in interpersonal situations. A score of 68–75 suggests high satisfaction, 58–67 indicates moderate satisfaction, while 45–57 shows that you feel dissatisfied with your communication behavior nearly half the time.

Another valuable way to use this activity is to make a second inventory at the end of the course. Have you improved? Are there still areas you will need to work on?

7

1.2 MEDIATED COMMUNICATION

LEARNING OBJECTIVES

- Describe the degree to which communication (in a specific instance or a relationship) is qualitatively impersonal or interpersonal, and describe the consequences of this level of interaction.
- Diagnose the effectiveness of various communication channels in a specific situation.
- Use the criteria in the chapter to determine the level of communication competence in a specific instance or a relationship.

INSTRUCTIONS

Answer the questions below. Then, in small or large group discussion compare your experiences with classmates.

1. List all the mediated channels you use to communicate interpersonally.

_____

_____

2. Describe the reasons you use mediated channels. Consider both *practical* reasons (e.g., to communicate over distance) and *strategic* ones (e.g., to avoid face-to-face confrontation).

_____

_____

3. Describe situations in which your communication is more effective using mediated channels and explain why.

_____

_____

4. Describe situations in which your communication is less effective using mediated channels and explain why.

_____

_____

5. How do you think relationships are affected when they begin through mediated communication rather than face-to-face?

_____

_____

6. What are the differences in the quantity, frequency, and quality of mediated communication you experience with different generations (parents, grandparents)? Do you use mediated communication more frequently with certain age-groups? Why or why not?

_____

_____

7. Your text cites a study that states that mediated communication encourages greater offline interaction with close friends. What is your experience? If you text message more, do you also see each other more?

_____

_____

8. Do you prefer mediated communication over face-to-face to meet some needs for information? Do you prefer e-mail, phone, text-messaging, or face-to-face communication with instructors, family, friends, co-workers, supervisors? Does this vary with the person's age, gender, role? How do you let others know your preferences?

_____

_____

9

1.3 COMMUNICATION BASICS

LEARNING OBJECTIVES

- Describe how the communication principles and misconceptions in Chapter 1 are evident in a specific situation.

- Assess the needs (physical, identity, social, and practical) that communicators are attempting to satisfy in a given situation or relationship.
- Apply the transactional communication model to a specific situation.

INSTRUCTIONS

Use the case below and the discussion questions that follow to discuss the variety of communication issues involved in effective communication. Make notes on this page, add other pages on your own, or prepare a group report/analysis based on your discussion. Add your own experiences to individualize the analysis.

CASE

Kristie and Jacob have been dating one another exclusively for four months. They both have part-time jobs and hope to complete their college studies within two years. Jacob thinks they should move in together. Kristie is reluctant to agree until she has more commitment from Jacob. Jacob doesn't want to make promises he can't keep. Kristie thinks that if they just communicate more they will be able to solve the problem, but Jacob thinks that talking about it more won't help.

1. What needs (physical, identity, social, and/or practical) do Kristie and Jacob seem to have?

_____

_____

2. Identify one element of the communication model that might help explain some of the communication problems they are having and help them communicate more effectively.

_____

_____

10

3. What communication principles and/or misconceptions described in Chapter 1 may be operating in this situation?

_____

_____

4. What likely role will mediated communication play in the scenario?

_____

_____

5. How would you advise Jacob and Kristie to proceed with their communication practices?

_____

_____

1.4 ASSESSING COMMUNICATION NEEDS

LEARNING OBJECTIVES
- Assess the needs (physical, identity, social, and practical) that communicators are attempting to satisfy in a given situation or relationship.

INSTRUCTIONS

Observe people in two other conversations, either in real life or on television. How did each individual attempt to meet their social, physical, identity, and practical needs during the conversation?
Use the checklist below in your analysis.

1) Physical needs: sufficient air, water, food, and rest and the ability to reproduce as a species

_____

_____

_____

2) Social needs: a link with others, involvement with others, control over the environment

_____

_____

_____

3) Identity needs: deciding who we are

_____

_____

_____

4) Practical goals: Which goals (if any) were being met through this interaction?

_____

_____

STUDY GUIDE

CHECK YOUR UNDERSTANDING

TRUE/FALSE

Mark the statements below as true or false. Correct false statements on the lines below to create a true statement.

_____ 1. Studies show your physical health may be affected by communication.

_____ 2. We learn who we are through communication with others and their reactions to us.

_____ 3. Communication skills are usually much less important in getting a job than technical competence, work experience, or a degree.

_____ 4. Instrumental goals are the same thing as social needs.

_____ 5. Psychologist Abraham Maslow claims that basic needs must be satisfied before people concern themselves with higher order needs.

_____ 6. The linear view of communication suggests that communication flows in one direction, from sender to receiver.

_____ 7. Disabled people have no repertoire of options available when responding to unwanted offers of help.

_____ 8. Richness is verbal cues that add clarity to a nonverbal message.

_____ 9. Disinhibition is speaking or transmitting messages without considering their consequences.

13

_____ 10. Dyadic communication is the earliest form of interaction we experience and the most common type of communication.

_____

_____ 11. What qualifies as competent behavior in one culture might be completely inept, or even offensive, in another.

_____

_____ 12. In order to build a competent relationship, we need to get rid of our need to maintain some space between ourselves and the other person.

_____

_____ 13. Ten minutes per day of socializing improves memory and boosts intellectual function.

_____

_____ 14. Research suggests that face-to-face relationships and virtual relationships are increasingly oppositional.

_____

_____ 15. MySpace, Facebook, and Twitter are just some of the ways that people can communicate through mediated channels.

_____

_____ 16. There is no place for impersonal communication in day to day activity.

_____

_____ 17. We can always choose not to communicate if the situation seems too difficult.

_____

COMPLETION

Fill in the blanks below with the correct terms chosen from the list below.

instrumental goals	social needs	identity needs	physiological noise
psychological noise	self-monitoring	co-cultures	richness
cognitive complexity	empathy		

1. _____ are the needs we have to define who we are.

2. _____ are the needs we have to link ourselves with others.

3. _____ are the needs we have to get others to behave in ways we want.

14

4. _____ refers to the forces within a communicator that interfere with the ability to express or understand a message accurately.

5. _____ refers to the biological factors in the receiver or sender that interfere with accurate reception of messages.

6. _____ groups that shape our perceptions: ethnic, national, religious

7. _____ is the abundance of nonverbal cues that add clarity to a verbal message.

8. _____ is the ability to construct a variety of different frameworks for viewing an issue.

9. _____ is the process of paying close attention to your behavior in order to shape the way you behave.

10. _____ is the ability to imagine how an issue might look from the other's point of view.

MULTIPLE CHOICE

Choose the letter of the communication process element that is most illustrated by the description found below. Italicized words provide clues.

a. encode
b. decode
c. channel
d. message/feedback
e. noise (external, physiological, or psychological)
f. environment

_____ 1. The children make a videotape of themselves to send to their grandparents instead of writing a letter.

_____ 2. Marjorie tries to decide the best way to tell Martin that she can't go to Hawaii with him.

_____ 3. Martin decides Marjorie means she doesn't love him when she says she can't go to Hawaii.

_____ 4. It's so hot in the room that Brad has a hard time concentrating on what his partner is telling him.

_____ 5. Linda smiles while Larry is talking to her.

_____ 6. Brooke is daydreaming about her date while Allison is talking to her.

15

_____ 7. Since Jacob has never been married, it's difficult for him to understand why his married friend Brent wants to spend less time with him.

_____ 8. Whitney says, "I'm positive about my vote."

_____ 9. Richard thinks Jon wants to leave when he waves to him.

_____ 10. Laura winks when she says she's serious and gestures with her arms.

_____ 11. Erin is from a wealthy family and Kate from a poor one. They have a serious conflict about how to budget their money.

_____ 12. Jack has been feeling a cold coming on all day while he has sat through the meeting.

Choose the *best* answer for each of the questions below:

13. The concept of co-cultures is closest to the concept of differing
    a. environments.
    b. relational messages.
    c. self-monitoring.
    d. impersonal communication.

14. Martin Buber's concept of communication that is truly interpersonal is called
    a. I-You.
    b. I-They.
    c. I-It.
    d. I-We.

15. Improving intercultural competence involves all of the following except
    a. motivation.
    b. open-mindedness.
    c. knowledge and skill.
    d. avoiding ambiguity.

16. According to the quantitative definition of interpersonal communication, interpersonal communication occurs when
    a. two people interact with one another, usually face to face.
    b. you watch a TV show about relationships.
    c. you read a romance novel.
    d. large numbers of people communicate.

17. All of the following statements are true <u>except</u>
    a. Communication has content and relational dimensions.
    b. Communication is irreversible.
    c. Communication can be unintentional.
    d. Communication is repeatable.

18. All of the following statements are true <u>except</u>
    a. Meanings are not in words.
    b. More communication is not always better.
    c. Communication can solve all your problems.
    d. Communication is not a natural ability.

19. According to most studies cited in your text, mediated communication
    a. diminishes the amount of face-to-face interaction.
    b. enriches and promotes more social interaction.
    c. leads to more impersonal communication in families.
    d. makes people more aware of gender and age differences.

20. When you are able to perform communication skills without thinking about how you should behave, you have entered the skill stage of
    a. awareness.
    b. awkwardness.
    c. skillfulness.
    d. integration.

21. When we volunteer personal information online that we prefer to keep private from some parties, this is one form of
    a. awareness.
    b. awkwardness.
    c. skillfulness.
    d. integration.

22. Communication competence seeks to be both
    a. loud and clear.
    b. effective and appropriate.
    c. skillful and concise.
    d. intuitive and cautious.

23. When using social media you should
    a. share your feelings openly and honestly.
    b. include everyone.

c. think before you post.

d. upload personal pictures.

24. In becoming a competent intercultural communicator you should
    a. trust the advice of friends.
    b. remain open-minded.
    c. use a linear communication model.
    d. minimize external noise

CHAPTER ONE STUDY GUIDE ANSWERS

TRUE/FALSE

1. T	4. F	7. F	10. T	13. T	16. F
2. T	5. T	8. F	11. T	14. F	17. F
3. F	6. T	9. T	12. F	15. T	

COMPLETION

1. identity needs
2. social needs
3. instrumental goals
4. psychological noise
5. physiological noise
6. co-cultures
7. richness
8. cognitive complexity
9. self-monitoring
10. empathy

MULTIPLE CHOICE

1. c	5. d	9. b	13. a	17. d	21. d
2. a	6. e	10. c	14. a	18. c	22. b.
3. b	7. f	11. f	15. d	19. b	23. c.
4. e	8. d	12. e	16. a	20. d.	24. b.

CHAPTER TWO

Communication and Identity: Creating and Presenting the Self

OUTLINE

Use this outline to take notes as you read the chapter in the text and/or as your instructor lectures in class.

I. COMMUNICATION AND THE SELF
  A. **Definitions**
     1. Self-concept
     2. Self-esteem
  B. **Biological and Social Roots of the Self**
     1. Personality
     2. Traits
     3. Socialization and the self-concept
       a. Reflected appraisal
       b. Significant others
       c. Social comparison
          i. superior/inferior
         ii. same/different
  C. **Characteristics of the Self-Concept**
     1. The self-concept is subjective
       a. obsolete information
       b. distorted feedback
       c. emphasis on perfection
       d. social expectations
     2. The self-concept resists change (cognitive conservatism)
	_____
	
	_____
	
	_____
	
	_____
	
	_____
	
	_____
	
	_____
	
	_____
	
	_____
	
	_____
	
	_____
	
	_____
	
	_____

         a.   have a realistic perception of
              yourself
         b.   have realistic expectations
         c.   have the will to change
         d.   have the skill to change
   D. **Culture, Gender, and Identity**
       1. Culture
          a. Individualistic
          b. Collectivistic
       2. Sex and gender
   E. **The Self-Fulfilling Prophecy and
       Communication**
       1.   Self-fulfilling prophecy
            a. holding an expectation
            b. behaving within expectations
            c. the expectation coming to
pass
            d. reinforcing the original
expectation
       2.   Types
            a.   self-imposed
            b.   imposed by others

II. **PRESENTING THE SELF:
     COMMUNICATION AS IDENTITY
     MANAGEMENT**
   A. **Public and Private Selves**
       1.   Perceived self
       2.   Presenting self (face)
   B. **Characteristics of Identity
       Management**
       1.   We construct multiple identities
       2.   Identity management is
            collaborative
       3.   Identity management can be
            deliberate or unconscious
   C.   **Why Manage Identities?**
       1.   To start and manage relationships
       2.   To gain the compliance of others

20

3. To save others' face
4. To explore new selves
D. **Managing Identities in Person and Online**
   1. Face-to-face identity management
      a. manner
      b. appearance
      c. setting
   2. Online impression management
      a. asynchronous mediated communication
      b. ideal online identity versus "real" self
      c. reputation management
E. **Identity Management and Honesty**
   1. Identity/impression management versus lying
   2. Situational behavior

III. **SELF-DISCLOSURE IN RELATIONSHIPS**
   A. **Definition**
   B. **Models of Self-Disclosure**
      1. Social penetration model
         a. breadth
         b. depth
      2. Johari Window
         a. open
         b. hidden
         c. blind
         d. unknown
   C. **Benefits and Risks of Self-Disclosure**
      1. Benefits of self-disclosure
         a. catharsis
         b. reciprocity
         c. self-clarification
         d. self-validation
         e. building and maintaining

relationships

       f. social influence

   2. Risks of self-disclosure

       a. rejection

       b. negative impression

       c. decrease in relational satisfaction

       d. loss of influence

       e. hurting the other person

  D. Guidelines for Self-Disclosure

    1.   Importance of the other to you

    2.   Appropriate amount and type

    3.   Reasonable risk

    4.   Constructive effects

    5.   Reciprocation

    6.   Moral obligation

IV. ALTERNATIVES TO SELF-DISCLOSURE

  A. Silence

  B. Lying

    1.   Benevolent lies

    2.   Reasons for lying

    3.   Effects of lies - threats to the relationship

  C. Equivocating

  D. Hinting

    1.   May prevent receiver or sender embarrassment

    2.   Hints may not be perceived

  E. The Ethics of Evasion

    1.   Motives

    2.   Effects

KEY TERMS

benevolent lies
breadth
cognitive conservatism
depth
face
identity management
Johari Window
perceived self
personality
presenting self
privacy management
reference groups
reflected appraisal
self-concept
self-disclosure
self-esteem
self-fulfilling prophecy
significant others
social comparison
social penetration

ACTIVITIES

2.1 WHO DO YOU THINK YOU ARE?

LEARNING OBJECTIVES

- Describe the relationship between self-concept, self-esteem, and communication.

- Explain how self-fulfilling prophecies shape the self-concept and influence communication.

- Demonstrate how the principles in the chapter can be used to change the self-concept, and hence communication.

INSTRUCTIONS

1. First, if possible, take a The Jung Typology Test at http://www.humanmetrics.com/cgi-win/JTypes2.asp. This will get you thinking about the way you describe yourself.
2. For each category below, supply the words or phrases that describe you best.
3. After filling in the spaces within each category, organize your responses so that the most fundamental characteristic is listed first, with the rest of the items following in order of descending importance.

PART A: IDENTIFY THE ELEMENTS OF YOUR SELF-CONCEPT

1. How would you describe your social behaviors (friendly, shy, aloof, talkative, etc.)?

   a. _____ b. _____ c. _____

2. How would you describe your personality traits (stable, extraverted, introverted, etc.)?

   a. _____ b. _____ c. _____

3. What beliefs do you hold strongly (vegetarian, green, Christian, pacifist, etc.)?

   a. _____ b. _____ c. _____

4. What social roles are the most important in your life (brother, student, friend, bank teller, club president, etc.)?

   a. _____ b. _____ c. _____

5. How would you describe your intellectual capacity (curious, poor reader, good mathematician, etc.)?

   a. _____ b. _____ c. _____

6. How would you describe your physical condition and/or your appearance (fit, sedentary, tall, attractive, etc.)?

   a. _____ b. _____ c. _____

7. What talents do you possess or lack (good artist, lousy carpenter, competent swimmer, etc.)?

   a. _____ b. _____ c. _____

8. What other descriptors are important to describe you (cultural, ethnic, gender, sexual orientation, moods, feelings, others)?

   a. _____ b. _____ c. _____

PART B: ARRANGE YOUR SELF-CONCEPT ELEMENTS IN ORDER OF IMPORTANCE

1. _____
2. _____
3. _____
4. _____
5. _____
6. _____
7. _____
8. _____
9. _____
10. _____
11. _____
12. _____
13. _____
14. _____
15. _____
16. _____
17. _____
18. _____
19. _____
20. _____

25

Describe any factors that have contributed in a positive or negative way to the formation of your perceived self. Explain if some were due to obsolete information, social expectations, distorted feedback, or perfection beliefs. Include any other factors involved in the formation of your perceived self (for example, certain significant others, any strong reference groups).

_____

_____

_____

_____

What significant others or reference groups contributed to your self-concept? How?

_____

_____

_____

_____

NOTE: You will use these descriptors in Activity 2.2.

2.2 SELF-CONCEPT INVENTORY

LEARNING OBJECTIVES

- Describe the relationship between self-concept, self-esteem, and communication.

- Compare and contrast the perceived self and the presenting self as they relate to identity management.

INSTRUCTIONS

1. Transfer the list of up to 20 elements of your self-concept from the previous exercise (2.1) to index cards (or strips of paper).
2. Arrange your cards in a stack, with the one that *best* describes you at the top and the one that *least* describes you at the bottom.
3. Record the order in which you arranged the cards (1 is the most like you) in the Perceived Self column (Column 1). You may leave out some cards or add on to your list.
4. Without revealing your Perceived Self column, ask two other people (a friend, co-worker, roommate, family member, classmate) to arrange the descriptors in an order in which they see you. Record these perceptions in Columns 2 and 3. Neither should see Column 1 or the other person's column. Record the name/relationship of your reviewers at the top of the appropriate column.
5. Compare the three tables, circling any descriptors that are exactly the same across the three columns. Highlight any that have similar ranks (no more than three numbers different).
6. Answer the questions at the end of this exercise.

Column 1 Perceived Self	Column 2 Presenting Self to _____ (relationship to you)	Column 3 Presenting Self to _____ (relationship to you)
1. _____	1. _____	1. _____
2. _____	2. _____	2. _____
3. _____	3. _____	3. _____
4. _____	4. _____	4. _____
5. _____	5. _____	5. _____
6. _____	6. _____	6. _____

7. _____	7. _____	7. _____
8. _____	8. _____	8. _____
9. _____	9. _____	9. _____
10. _____	10. _____	10. _____
11. _____	11. _____	11. _____
12. _____	12. _____	12. _____
13. _____	13. _____	13. _____
14. _____	14. _____	14. _____
15. _____	15. _____	15. _____
16. _____	16. _____	16. _____
17. _____	17. _____	17. _____
18. _____	18. _____	18. _____
19. _____	19. _____	19. _____
20. _____	20. _____	20. _____

Describe any differences between your perceived self and the ways your reviewers perceived you (your presenting selves). What factors contribute to the differences in perception? Whose view is the most accurate and why?

_____

_____

_____

_____

_____

Why might your reviewers in this exercise view you differently from the way you perceive yourself? Would other people in your life view you like either of the people in this exercise? Give some specific examples with reasons why they would or would not have a similar perception.

_____

_____

_____

_____

_____

2.3 EGO BOOSTERS AND BUSTERS

LEARNING OBJECTIVES

- Describe the relationship between self-concept, self-esteem, and communication.
- Demonstrate how the principles in Chapter 2 can be used to change the self-concept, and hence communication.
- Compare and contrast the perceived self and the presenting self as they relate to identity management.

INSTRUCTIONS

1. In the appropriate spaces below describe the actions of several "ego boosters": significant others who shaped your self-concept in a positive way. Also describe the behavior of "ego busters" who contributed to a more negative self-concept.
2. Next, recall several incidents in which you behaved as an ego booster or buster to others. Not all ego boosters and busters are obvious. Include in your description several incidents in which the messages were **subtle or nonverbal**.
3. Summarize the lessons you have learned from this experience by answering the questions at the end of this exercise.

EGO BOOSTER MESSAGES YOU HAVE RECEIVED

EXAMPLE

I perceive(d) _my communication lab partner_ **(significant other)** as telling me I am/was

attractive **(self-concept element)** when he or she kept _sneaking glances at me and smiling during our taping project._

1. I perceived _____ (significant other) as telling me I am/was

   _____ (self-concept element) when he/she _____

   _____

   _____

2. I perceived _____ (significant other) as telling me I am/was

_____ (self-concept element) when he/she _____

_____

_____

EGO BUSTER MESSAGES YOU HAVE RECEIVED

EXAMPLE

I perceive(d) _my neighbor_ (significant other) as telling me I am/was _not an important friend_ (self-concept element) when he/she _had a big party last weekend and didn't invite me._

1. I perceived _____ (significant other) as telling me I am/was

_____(self-concept element) when he/she _____

_____

_____

2. I perceived _____ (significant other) as telling me I am/was

_____(self-concept element) when he/she _____

_____

_____

EGO BOOSTER MESSAGES YOU HAVE SENT

EXAMPLE

I was a booster to _my instructor_ when I _told her I enjoyed last Tuesday's lecture._

1. I was a booster to _____ when I _____

_____

_____

31

2. I was a booster to _____ when I _____

_____

_____

EGO BUSTER MESSAGES YOU HAVE SENT

EXAMPLE

I was a buster to _my sister_ when I _forgot to phone her or send even a card on her birthday._

1. I was a buster to _____ when I _____

_____

2. I was a buster to _____ when I _____

_____

CONCLUSIONS

Who are the people who have most influenced your self-concept in the past? What messages did each one send to influence you so strongly?

_____

_____

_____

What people are the greatest influences on your self-concept now? Is each person a positive or a negative influence? What messages does each one send to influence your self-concept?

_____

_____

_____

_____

Who are the people whom *you* have influenced greatly? What messages have you sent to each one about his or her self-concept? How have you sent these messages?

_____

_____

_____

_____

What ego booster or buster messages do you want to send to the important people in your life? How (with what channels) can you send each one?

_____

_____

_____

GROUP DISCUSSION

After completing the first part of this activity individually, share some of your answers with a small group of classmates. Then, as a group, answer the questions on the next page.

1. What channels are most important for you to receive ego boosters? or buster messages do you want to send to the important people in your life? How (with what channels) can you send each one?

_____

_____

2. What channels are most often used for ego busters that are unintentional? What advice would you have in order to avoid inadvertently sending ego busters?

_____

_____

_____

3. After reviewing your experiences, what advice would you give to supervisors regarding ego boosters and ego busters?

_____

_____

_____

4. After reviewing your experiences, what advice would you give to parents regarding ego boosters and ego busters?

_____

_____

_____

2.4 REEVALUATING YOUR "CAN'TS"

LEARNING OBJECTIVES

- Explain how self-fulfilling prophecies shape the self-concept and influence communication.

INSTRUCTIONS

1. Complete the following lists by describing communication-related difficulties you have in the following areas.
2. After filling in each blank space, follow the starred instructions that follow the list (*).

DIFFICULTIES YOU HAVE COMMUNICATING WITH FAMILY MEMBERS

EXAMPLES

I can't *discuss politics with my dad without having an argument* because *he's so set in his ways.*
I can't *tell my brother how much I love him* because *I'll feel foolish.*

1. I can't _____

    because _____

2. I can't _____

    because _____

* Corrections (see instructions at end of exercise)

_____

DIFFICULTIES YOU HAVE COMMUNICATING WITH PEOPLE AT SCHOOL OR AT WORK

EXAMPLES

I can't *say "no" when my boss asks me to work overtime*
because *he'll fire me.*
I can't *participate in class discussions even when I know the answers or have a question*
because *I just freeze up.*

1. I can't _____

because _____

2. I can't _____

    because _____

* Corrections (see instructions at end of exercise)

_____

_____

DIFFICULTIES YOU HAVE COMMUNICATING WITH STRANGERS

EXAMPLES

I can't *start a conversation with someone I've never met before*
because *I'll look stupid.*
I can't *ask smokers to move or stop smoking*
because *they'll get mad.* _____

1. I can't _____

    because _____

2. I can't _____

    because _____

* Corrections (see instructions at end of exercise)

_____

_____

DIFFICULTIES YOU HAVE COMMUNICATING WITH FRIENDS

EXAMPLES

I can't *find the courage to ask my friend to repay the money he owes me*
because *I'm afraid he'll question our friendship.*
I can't *say no when friends ask me to do favors and I'm busy*
because *I'm afraid they'll think I'm not their friend.* _____

1. I can't _____

    because _____

2. I can't _____

   because _____

* Corrections (see instructions at end of exercise)

_____

_____

DIFFICULTIES YOU HAVE COMMUNICATING WITH YOUR ROMANTIC PARTNER (PAST OF PRESENT)

EXAMPLES

I can't *tell Bill to wear a tie to the party*
because *he'll laugh at me.*
I can't *bring up going to visit my parents*
because *we'll fight.*

1. I can't _____

   because _____

2. I can't _____

   because _____

* Corrections (see instructions at end of exercise)

_____

PREDICTIONS MADE BY OTHERS

EXAMPLES

You'll never amount to anything.   You can't expect much with your background.
You're just like your father.   The James children never were too bright.

1. _____

2. _____

* Corrections (see instructions at end of exercise)

_____

*After you have completed the list, continue as follows:
   a.   Read the list you have made. Actually say each item to yourself and note your feelings.

37

b. Now read the list again, but with a slight difference. For each "can't," substitute the word "won't" or "until now I've chosen not to." For instance, "I can't say no to friends' requests" becomes "I won't say no" or "Until now I've chosen not to say no." Circle any statements that are actually "won'ts" or choices.

c. Read the list for a third time. For this repetition substitute "I don't know how" or "I haven't yet learned to" for your original "can't." Instead of saying "I can't approach strangers," say, "I don't know how to approach strangers." *Correct* your original list to show which statements are truly "don't know how" or "haven't yet learned" statements

d. For the "Predictions made by others " substitute your strength(s) which makes the prediction untrue (example: "I am my father's child, but I can choose not to repeat behaviors he has that I don't like.").

After completing this exercise, consider how greater awareness of the power that negative self-fulfilling prophecies have on your self-concept and thus on your communication behavior. Imagine how differently you would behave if you eliminated any incorrect uses of the word "can't" from your thinking.

2.5 MEDIATED MESSAGES – IDENTITY MANAGEMENT

LEARNING OBJECTIVES

- Compare and contrast the perceived self and the presenting self as they relate to identity management.

- Describe the role that identity management plays in both face-to-face and mediated relationships.

INSTRUCTIONS

Discuss each of the questions below in your group. For each question, take a minute of silence and let each person jot down some notes. Then go around and let each person share something. Then have a more extended discussion and if directed by your instructor, prepare to report your group's conclusions back to the whole class.

1. Describe ways in which messages from the mass media (i.e., music, television, film, magazines, books) have contributed to your self-concept or the self-concepts of people you know well.

_____

_____

2. Your text states that people often prefer mediated channels when their self-presentation is threatened (delivering bad news, declining invitations). Do your experiences refute or validate this conclusion? Give examples.

_____

_____

3. Identity management is important in mediated contexts. Describe how you manage identity in any mediated contexts you use (online dating services, written notes, e-mail, e-mail address, instant messaging, blogging, personal ads, web pages).

_____

_____

4. Do you prefer to meet people online or face-to-face initially? Why? Is your answer the same or different for friendships than for work or career situations? Why?

_____

2.6 ASSESSING IDENTITY MANAGEMENT

LEARNING OBJECTIVES

- Compare and contrast the perceived self and the presenting self as they relate to identity management.

INSTRUCTIONS

Think of the many identities you have, such as friend, daughter, athlete, etc. Label and describe your presenting or public self in each situation. Describe how you manage them in the following situations. In the identity spaces below, list one of the identities you manage and describe the communication strategies you use to influence how others view you.

Identity #1 _____

At school:

_____

_____

_____

Identity #2 _____

With your family:

_____

_____

_____

Identity #3 _____

At work:

_____

_____

_____

Identity # 4 _____

Online:

_____

_____

_____

2.7 BREADTH AND DEPTH OF RELATIONSHIPS

LEARNING OBJECTIVES

- Identify the dimensions of intimacy that operate and how they are expressed in a specific relationship.
- Explain the need for both intimacy and distance in a given relationship.
- Use the social penetration and Johari Window models to identify the nature of self-disclosing communication in one of your relationships.
- Outline the potential benefits and risks of disclosing in a selected situation.

INSTRUCTIONS

1. Use the form below to make a social penetration model for a significant relationship you have, indicating the depth and breadth of various areas. See Figure 2.3 and 2.7 in Chapter 2 of *Looking Out/Looking In* for an example of the social penetration model.
2. Answer the questions at the end of the exercise.

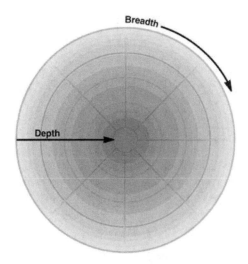

Social Penetration Model

Significant relationship described: _____

CONCLUSIONS

How deep or shallow is your relationship with this person?

_____

_____

Does the depth vary from one area (breadth) to another? In what way?

_____

_____

_____

Are you satisfied with the depth and breadth of this relationship? Why or why not?

_____

_____

_____

If you are not satisfied, what could you do to change the relationship? What would you predict the results would be?

_____

_____

_____

_____

_____

_____

_____

_____

43

2.8 REASONS FOR NONDISCLOSURE

LEARNING OBJECTIVES

- Use the social penetration and Johari Window models to identify the nature of self-disclosing communication in one of your relationships.
- Outline the potential benefits and risks of disclosing in a selected situation.

INSTRUCTIONS

1. Choose a particular individual about whom you want to analyze your self-disclosing behavior.
2. In the column to the left of each item, indicate the extent to which you use each reason to avoid disclosing.

   5 = almost always   2 = rarely
   4 = often   1 = never
   3 = sometimes

3. In the column to the right of each item, indicate how reasonable and realistic the reason is.

   5 = totally realistic
   4 = mostly realistic
   3 = partly realistic, partly unrealistic
   2 = mostly unrealistic
   1 = totally unrealistic

How Frequently Do You Use the Reason?		How Realistic and Rational Is the Reason?
_____	1. I can't find the opportunity to self-disclose with this person.	_____
_____	2. If I disclose I might hurt the other person.	_____
_____	3. If I disclose I might be evaluating or judging the person.	_____
_____	4. I can't think of topics that I would disclose.	_____
_____	5. Self-disclosure would give information that might be used against me at some time.	_____
_____	6. If I disclose it might cause me to make personal changes.	_____
_____	7. Self-disclosure might threaten relationships I have with people other than the close acquaintance to whom I disclose.	_____

How Frequently Do You Use		How Realistic and Rational

_____   8.   Self-disclosure is a sign of weakness.   _____

_____   9.   If I disclose I might lose control over the other person.   _____

_____   10.   If I disclose I might discover I am less than I wish to be.   _____

_____   11.   If I disclose I might project an image I do not want to project.   _____

_____   12.   If I disclose the other person might not understand what
                  I was saying.   _____

_____   13.   If I disclose the other person might evaluate me negatively.   _____

_____   14.   Self-disclosure is a sign of some emotional disturbance.   _____

_____   15.   Self-disclosure might hurt our relationship.   _____

_____   16.   I am afraid that self-disclosure might lead to an intimate
                  relationship with the other person.   _____

_____   17.   Self-disclosure might threaten my physical safety.   _____

_____   18.   If I disclose I might give information that makes me
                  appear inconsistent.   _____

_____   19.   Any other reasons: _____   _____

*Based on a survey developed by Lawrence B. Rosenfeld, "Self-Disclosure Avoidance: Why Am I Afraid to Tell You Who I Am?" *Communication Monographs* 46 (1979): 63–74.

What does this personal survey tell you about your thoughts and feelings about self-disclosure with this person?

_____

_____

_____

Do you think your level of self-disclosure is appropriate or inappropriate with this person? Why or why not?

_____

_____

How would you summarize and categorize the major reasons that you self-disclose using these categories: Catharsis, Reciprocity, Self-clarification, Self-validation, Identity management, Relational maintenance, Social influence?

_____

_____

_____

How different would your survey look if you'd chosen a different relationship? Why?

_____

_____

2.9 DEGREES OF SELF-DISCLOSURE

LEARNING OBJECTIVES

- Use the social penetration and Johari Window models to identify the nature of self-disclosing communication in one of your relationships.
- Outline the potential benefits and risks of disclosing in a selected situation.

INSTRUCTIONS

For each of the following topics, write two statements for each level of self-disclosure. (See Chapter 2 of *Looking Out/Looking In* for descriptions of each level.)

EXAMPLE

Topic: School

1. Clichés
   a. *Finals are no fun!*
   b. *Textbooks sure are expensive!*
2. Facts
   a. *I'm a psychology major at the university.*
   b. *I'm getting a teaching certificate so I'll be able to teach social studies.*
3. Opinions
   a. *I think people over 18 should be allowed to keep a driver's license if they don't vote.*
   b. *I don't think instructors should count attendance as part of a person's grade.*

4. Feelings
   a. *I feel scared when I think about the future. I'm almost finished with four years of college, and I'm*
      still confused about what to do with my life.
   b. *I get angry when Professor Autel doesn't prepare adequately for our class.*

TOPIC: MY FAMILY

1. Clichés

   a. _____

   b. _____

2. Facts

   a. _____

b. _____

3. Opinions

    a. _____

    b. _____

4. Feelings

    a. _____

    b. _____

TOPIC: MY CAREER PLANS

1. Clichés

    a. _____

    b. _____

2. Facts

    a. _____

    b. _____

3. Opinions

    a. _____

    b. _____

4. Feelings

    a. _____

    b. _____

TOPIC: POLITICS

1. Clichés

    a. _____

b. _____

2. Facts

   a. _____

   b. _____

3. Opinions

   a. _____

   b. _____

4. Feelings

   a. _____

   b. _____

TOPIC: SPORTS

1. Clichés

   a. _____

   b. _____

2. Facts

   a. _____

   b. _____

3. Opinions

   a. _____

   b. _____

4. Feelings

   a. _____

   b. _____

2.10 DISCLOSURE AND ALTERNATIVES

LEARNING OBJECTIVES

- Use the social penetration and Johari Window models to identify the nature of self-disclosing communication in one of your relationships.
- Outline the potential benefits and risks of disclosing in a selected situation.
- Assess the most competent mixture of candor and equivocation in a given situation.

INSTRUCTIONS

1. For each situation described below, record responses for the types listed.
2. Evaluate the effectiveness and ethics of your responses.
3. Describe a disclosure situation of your own in the same manner.

EXAMPLE

Your friend asks you if you had a good time when you went out with his cousin last night.
Self-disclosure: *I didn't have a great time, but then we were just getting to know one another. I don't think that we had much in common.*
Silence: *If I don't answer or don't say anything, my friend might think it was worse than I do.*
Lying: *Your cousin was a lot of fun and the movie was great.*
Equivocating: *First dates are really times of discovery, aren't they?*
Hinting: *I don't think I have to have a great time every night.*
Which response is most effective/which most ethical? *I think equivocating is effective.*
While I wasn't exactly self-disclosing with my friend, I just don't want to tell him how boring I think his cousin is. I haven't lied and both of them can save face, too.

1. After your romantic partner has a bad week at work, his/her boss asks you how he/she is feeling about the company.

   Self-Disclosure _____

   Silence _____

   Lying _____

   Equivocating _____

   Hinting _____

   Which responses are most effective/which most ethical? _____

   _____

   _____

2. You are applying to rent an apartment that prohibits animals. You have a cat.

   Self-Disclosure _____

   Silence _____

   Lying _____

   Equivocating _____

   Hinting _____

   Which responses are most effective/which most ethical? _____

   _____

   _____

3. Your siblings ask you about your financial status (which is much better than theirs).

   Self-Disclosure _____

   Silence _____

   Lying _____

   Equivocating _____

   Hinting _____

   Which responses are most effective/which most ethical? _____

   _____

   _____

4. Your roommates ask what you think of the bright posters they've just put up around the living room.

   Self-Disclosure _____

   Silence _____

   Lying _____

   Equivocating _____

   Hinting _____

Which responses are most effective/which most ethical? _____

_____

_____

5. Your romantic partner asks how many other people you've really loved before you met him or her.

Self-Disclosure _____

Silence _____

Lying _____

Equivocating _____

Hinting _____

Which responses are most effective/which most ethical? _____

_____

_____

6. Your very opinionated father, whose opinions differ from yours, asks what you think of the person running for governor.

Self-Disclosure _____

Silence _____

Lying _____

Equivocating _____

Hinting _____

Which responses are most effective/which most ethical? _____

_____

_____

7. Your boss wants to know what your plans for the future are; you're looking around.

Self-Disclosure _____

Silence _____

Lying _____

Equivocating _____

Hinting _____

Which responses are most effective/which most ethical? _____

_____

_____

8. Your mother asks you about what your brother has been up to lately. You know he is probably moving out of state in a few months but he doesn't want your mom to know yet.

Self-Disclosure _____

Silence _____

Lying _____

Equivocating _____

Hinting _____

Which responses are most effective/which most ethical? _____

_____

_____

9. Your example: _____

Self-Disclosure _____

Silence _____

Lying _____

Equivocating _____

Hinting _____

Which responses are most effective/which most ethical? _____

STUDY GUIDE

CHECK YOUR UNDERSTANDING

TRUE/FALSE

Mark the statements below as true or false. Correct statements that are false on the lines below to create a true statement.

_____ 1. Collaboration in identity management means absolute agreement about each person's role.

_____

_____ 2. Most researchers agree that we are born with a fully formed self-concept.

_____

_____ 3. Some studies show that people strongly influenced by media body images develop more negative self-images.

_____

_____ 4. Self-fulfilling prophecies can affect job performance.

_____

_____ 5. Research has shown that people with high self-esteem seek out partners who view them unfavorably because they are strong enough to take the criticism.

_____

_____ 6. Personality is flexible, dynamic, and shaped by experiences.

_____

_____ 7. In individualistic societies, there is a higher degree of communication apprehension.

_____

_____ 8. The self-concept is such a powerful force that it not only influences how you see yourself in the present but also can actually influence your future behavior and that of others.

_____

_____ 9. Research shows that people who believe they are incompetent are more likely than others to pursue rewarding relationships in an attempt to ally themselves with competent people.

_____

_____ 10. High self-monitors feel less intimacy, satisfaction, and commitment in their romantic relationships because they do not hide what they really feel.

_____ 11. Trying on a "new self" can be a means to self-improvement.

_____ 12. Self-esteem has little to do with self-worth evaluations.

COMPLETION

Fill in the blanks below with the correct terms chosen from the list below.

distorted feedback	obsolete information	self-delusion
ego booster	ego buster	realistic expectations
realistic perceptions	manner	self-fulfilling prophecy
appearance		

1. _____ is someone who helps enhance your self-esteem by acting in ways that make you feel accepted, important, and loved.

2. _____ is someone who acts to reduce your self-esteem.

3. _____ are messages that others send to you that are unrealistically positive or negative.

4. _____ consists of a communicator's words and nonverbal actions that help create an impression.

5. _____ is information that was once true about you that is no longer true.

6. _____ are the personal items people use to shape an image.

7. _____ is the inability to see a real need for change in the self, due to holding an unrealistically favorable picture of yourself.

8. _____ are reasonable goals to set for self-growth.

9. _____ occurs when expectations of an event influences a person's behavior, which in turn influences the event's outcome.

10. _____ are relatively accurate views of the strengths and weaknesses of the self.

MULTIPLE CHOICE

Identify which principle influences the self-concept in each example.

   a. obsolete information
   b. distorted feedback
   c. emphasis on perfection
   d. social expectations

_____ 1. You always scored more points than anyone else on your team in high school. You still think you're the best even though your college teammates are scoring more than you.

_____ 2. You keep getting down on yourself because you can't cook as well as Megan, even though you are a great student and a fair athlete.

_____ 3. You believe people shouldn't brag or boast, so you tell others that you "blew" the chemistry test and got a "C–" but you never acknowledge your "A's" in math.

_____ 4. Your parents tell you, their friends, and all your relatives about all your wonderful accomplishments, even though you have only average achievement.

_____ 5. Janee says that you are insensitive to her perspective despite your many attempts to listen honestly to her and empathize.

_____ 6. You pay a lot of attention to the magazines showing perfectly dressed and groomed individuals and keep wishing you could look as good as they do.

_____ 7. You think of yourself as the shy fifth grader despite being at the social hub of at least three clubs on campus.

_____ 8. You feel uncomfortable accepting the compliments your friends honestly give you.

_____ 9. You're exhausted by trying to get all A's, work 30 hours a week, and be a loving romantic partner at the same time. You don't see how so many other people manage to get it all done.

_____ 10. "You're the perfect weight," your father tells you despite your recent gain of twenty pounds over the normal weight for your height.

Choose the *best* answer for each statement below:

11. Deciding which part of your self-concept to reveal to others is termed
   a. prophecy.
   b. impression management.
   c. collectivism.
   d. two-faced syndrome.

12. The most significant part of a person's self-concept
    a. is the social roles the person plays.
    b. is his or her appearance.
    c. is his or her accomplishments.
    d. is different for different people.

13. Self-esteem has to do with evaluations of
    a. self-concept.
    b. self-image.
    c. self-worth.
    d. self-discovery.

14. Which of the following could be an example of a self-fulfilling prophecy?
    a. Sid is born with a very large nose.
    b. Margarita has a very large, extended family.
    c. Serge is a Russian immigrant.
    d. Joy has given up on trying to talk to her unreasonable father.

15. The fact that none of us can see ourselves completely accurately illustrates the _____ nature of the self-concept.
    a. subjective
    b. objective
    c. unrealistic
    d. verification

16. Which of the following statements about gender and self-concept is correct?
    a. Women struggle with self-esteem issues more than men.
    b. Men's sense of superiority tends to decrease over time.
    c. Men tend to have low appraisals of their leadership and athletic abilities.
    d. Women tend to have high appraisals of their leadership and athletic abilities.

17. The influence of significant others
    a. is the sole determinant of our self-concept.
    b. becomes less powerful as people grow older.
    c. is synonymous with the term reflected appraisal.
    d. only occurs in people with poor self-concepts.

18. Computer-mediated communication
    a. makes it impossible to manage identity.
    b. has only disadvantages for impression management.
    c. can be an effective tool for impression management.
    d. always lessens the amount of interpersonal communication.

19. Which is the fourth stage of a self-fulfilling prophecy?
    a. holding an expectation (for yourself or for others)
    b. behaving in accordance with that expectation
    c. the expectation coming to pass
    d. reinforcing the original expectation

20. Communicating ego busters to others would seem to violate which concept of moral rules theory?
    a. nonmaleficence
    b. self-improvement
    c. justice
    d. gratitude

CHAPTER TWO STUDY GUIDE ANSWERS

TRUE/FALSE

1. F	5. F	9. F	
2. T	6. T	10. F	
3. T	7. F	11. T	
4. T	8. T	12. F	

COMPLETION

1. ego booster
2. ego buster
3. distorted feedback
4. manner

5. obsolete information
6. appearance
7. self-delusion
8. realistic expectations

9. self-fulfilling prophecy
10. realistic perceptions

MULTIPLE CHOICE

1. a	5. b	9. c	13. c	17. b
2. c	6. c	10. b	14. d	18. c
3. d	7. a	11. b	15. a	19. d
4 b	8. d	12. d	16. a	20. a

CHAPTER THREE

Perception: What You See Is What You Get

OUTLINE

Use this outline to take notes as you read the chapter in the text and/or as your instructor lectures in class.

I. **THE PERCEPTION PROCESS**

  A. **Selection** is influenced by

    1. Intense stimuli

    2. Repetitious stimuli

    3. Contrast or change in stimulation

    4. Motives

  B. **Organization**

    1. Figure–ground organization

    2. Perceptual schema

      a. appearance

      b. social roles

      c. interaction style

      d. psychological traits

      e. membership

    3. Stereotyping

    4. Punctuation

  C. **Interpretation**

    1. Degree of involvement with the other person

    2. Personal experience

    3. Assumptions about human behavior

    4. Attitudes

        5. Expectations
        6. Knowledge
        7. Self-concept
        8. Relational satisfaction
    D. **Negotiation**
        1. Narratives tell our stories
        2. Narratives may clash
        3. Shared narratives

II. **INFLUENCES ON PERCEPTION**
    A. **Access to Information**
        1. Roles
        2. Social media
    B. **Physiological Influences**
        1. Senses
        2. Psychological challenges
        3. Age
        4. Health and fatigue
        5. Hunger
        6. Biological cycles
    B. **Cultural Differences**
        1. Worldview
        2. Value of talk and silence
        3. Ethnocentrism
        4. Subcultures
    C. **Social Roles**
        1. Gender roles (masculine, feminine, androgynous, undifferentiated)
        2. Occupational roles
        3. Relational roles

III. **COMMON TENDENCIES IN PERCEPTION**
    A. **We Judge Ourselves More Charitably Than Others**
    B. **We Cling to First Impressions**
    C. **We Assume Others Are Similar to Us**

60

D. **We Are Influenced by Our Expectations**

E. **We Are Influenced by the Obvious**

IV. **PERCEPTION CHECKING**

    A. **Elements of Perception Checking**

        1. Describe behavior

        2. Interpret behavior two ways

        3. Request clarification

    B. **Perception-Checking Considerations**

        1. Completeness

        2. Nonverbal congruency

        3. Cultural rules

            a. low-context cultures

            b. high-context cultures

        4. Face saving

V. **EMPATHY, COGNITIVE COMPLEXITY, AND COMMUNICATION**

    A. **Empathy**

        1. Definition

            a. perspective taking

            b. emotional dimension

            c. genuine concern

        2. Social intelligence

        3. Cultural considerations

        4. Sympathy

    B. **Cognitive Complexity**

        1. Communication

        2. Increasing cognitive complexity: the pillow method

        a. Position One: I'm right, you're wrong

        b. Position Two: You're right, I'm wrong

        c. Position Three: Both right, both wrong

d. Position Four: The issue isn't as important as it seems e. Position Five: There is truth in all four perspectives	

KEY TERMS

androgynous
attribution
empathy
ethnocentrism
gender role
halo effect
interpretation
narrative
negotiation

organization
perception checking
pillow method
punctuation
selection
self-serving bias
stereotyping
sympathy

ACTIVITIES

3.1 GUARDING AGAINST PERCEPTUAL ERRORS

LEARNING OBJECTIVES

- Explain how the influences on perception listed in this chapter affect communication in a specific situation.
- Analyze how the tendencies described in this chapter have distorted your perceptions of another person, and hence your communication. Use this information to present a more accurate alternative set of perceptions.

INSTRUCTIONS

1. Identify two people about whom you've formed strong opinions. These opinions can be positive or negative. In either case, describe them.
2. Using the checklist provided, comment on the accuracy or inaccuracy of your perceptions of each person. See Chapter 3 of *Looking Out/Looking In* for a more detailed description of the checklist factors. NOTE: Not every factor may apply to each person.
3. Record your conclusions at the end of the exercise.
4. Compare your examples with those of other classmates.

	Example	PERSON A	PERSON B
Identify each person. Describe your opinions.	Joni is my wife's good friend. I don't like her; I think she's boring. Her voice is shrill, and I find her annoying.		
1. We judge ourselves more charitably than others.	When Joni lost her job, I thought it was Joni's fault because she's so annoying. Of course, when I got laid off a few months later, I blamed the economy and mentioned nothing about my performance or personality.		

63

	Example	PERSON A	PERSON B
2. We pay more attention to other's negative characteristics.	Joni is attractive, intelligent, successful, and athletic. I tend to disregard all those positive qualities and focus on her shrill voice.		
3. We are influenced by the obvious.	Because she's my wife's friend, Joni is around a lot, so I probably notice her voice or her calls more than is usual.		
4. We cling to first impressions.	I haven't liked Joni from the beginning. She would call right at our dinner time. Even though she doesn't do this anymore, I still remember it and I'm sure it influences my opinion of her.		
5. We tend to assume that others are similar to us.	I just assume that Joni will know when I don't want her around. I assume she'd be interested in things I'm interested in. Perhaps she finds the topics I talk about boring, too.		

CONCLUSIONS

Based on the observations above, how accurate or inaccurate are your perceptions of other people?

_____

_____

_____

_____

64

What might you do in the future to guard against inaccurate perceptions of people?

_____

_____

_____

_____

3.2 SHIFTING PERSPECTIVES (PILLOW METHOD)

LEARNING OBJECTIVES

- Enhance your cognitive complexity by applying the "pillow method" in a significant disagreement. Explain how your expanded view of this situation might affect your communication with the other(s) involved.

INSTRUCTIONS

1. Select one disagreement or other issue that is now affecting an interpersonal relationship. This might be an issue such as "I think our children should go to public school; my spouse wants them to go to private school" or a more public disagreement such as "I think voting for a third party helps democracy in our country; my friend thinks it undermines democracy by drawing votes away from the two major parties."
2. Record enough background information for an outsider to understand your stance on the issue. Who is involved? How long has the disagreement been going on? What are the basic issues involved?
3. Describe the issue from each of the four positions listed below.
4. Record your conclusions at the end of this exercise.

OPTIONS

Create diverse groups of four; try to have gender, age, and ethnic diversity if possible. Let each person jot down a few notes about a disagreement and the four positions. Now, have one person at a time describe his/her situation and the first position. For each of the other positions, the other group members can help the speaker see even more ways to view the situation from other perspectives.

With a partner, role-play your situation orally for the class.

Brief Background Information

_____

_____

_____

_____

Position 1: "I'm right and you're wrong." Explain how you are right and the other person is wrong.

_____

_____

_____

_____

_____

_____

Position 2: "You're right and I'm wrong." Explain how the other person's position is correct, or at least understandable.

_____

_____

_____

_____

_____

Position 3: "We're both right and we're both wrong." Show that there are both correct (or understandable) and mistaken (or unreasonable) parts of both positions.

_____

_____

_____

_____

_____

Position 4: "The issue may be less important than it seems; some other things may be more important." Describe at least two ways in which the elements developed in positions 1–3 might affect your relationship. Describe at least one way in which the issue might be seen as less important than it was originally and describe at least one way in which the issue might be seen as more important than it was originally.

_____

_____

CONCLUSION

1. Explain how there is some truth in each of the preceding positions.

_____

_____

_____

_____

_____

_____

2. Explain how viewing the issue from each of the preceding positions might change your perception of the issue and how it might change your behavior in the future.

_____

_____

_____

_____

_____

_____

3. Explain how this issue and your understanding of it affect your relationship.

_____

_____

_____

_____

_____

_____

4. Explain the impact of hearing classmates explain how you might view the issue differently.

_____

_____

_____

_____

_____

_____

69

3.3 PERCEPTION-CHECKING PRACTICE

LEARNING OBJECTIVES

- Describe how the processes of selection, organization, interpretation, and negotiation shape communication in a given situation.
- Explain how the influences on perception listed in this chapter affect communication in a specific situation.
- Demonstrate how you might use the skill of perception checking in a significant relationship.

INSTRUCTIONS

1. Alone or with a partner, write a perception check for each of the situations below or spontaneously create an oral perception check. If you write them first, practice delivering them aloud to each other.

EXAMPLE

Yesterday your friend Erin laughed at a joke about "dumb blonds." You found it offensive.

Perception-checking statement: *Erin, when Joey cracked the dumb blond joke last night, you laughed. I'm wondering if you disapproved of the joke but laughed just to make Joey feel comfortable, or if you really think that blonds are not as smart as the rest of the population. Can you clarify things for me?*

1. Last night you saw a recent date walking on the beach, holding hands with someone. You'd like to date again, but don't want to if a current relationship exists. You get a call from the recent date, asking you to a movie and dinner this weekend.

_____

_____

_____

_____

2. Ever since the school year began, your father has called weekly, asking how you are doing. He's just called and asked again.

_____

_____

_____

_____

3. Your friend was driving you home from a party last night when he began to weave the car between lanes on the highway. You were uncomfortable, but didn't say anything then. Now it is the next morning and he shows up to take you to a class. You have decided to bring up the incident.

_____

_____

_____

_____

4. For the last two weeks, when you are leaving your house, your roommate has asked for a ride somewhere. Your roommate has a car, but you haven't seen it lately. You are in a hurry now, and your roommate has just asked for another ride.

_____

_____

_____

_____

5. You return home at night to find your roommate reading on the couch. When you walk into the room and greet him, he grunts and turns his face away from you and keeps reading.

_____

_____

_____

_____

6. Last week your instructor returned your exam with a low grade and the comment, "This kind of work paints a bleak picture for the future." You have approached the instructor to discuss the remark.

_____

_____

_____

_____

7. In one of your regular long distance phone conversations you ask your favorite cousin about his romantic life. He sighs and says, "Oh, it's OK, I guess."

_____

_____

_____

_____

8. Your girlfriend, boyfriend, or spouse announces that she or he plans to spend next Friday night with friends from work. You usually spend Friday nights with each other.

_____

_____

_____

_____

9. Last week your supervisor at work, Ms. Black, gave you a big assignment. Three times since then she has asked you whether you're having any trouble with it.

_____

_____

_____

_____

10. Last weekend your next-door neighbor, Steve, raked a big pile of leaves near your property line, promising to clean them up after work on Monday. It's Wednesday, and the wind is blowing the leaves into your yard.

_____

_____

_____

_____

11. One of your classmates sits by you every day in class and you've done a lot of homework together; he's called you at home a few times a week. He suggests that you meet for dinner this weekend.

_____

_____

_____

_____

12. You've noticed one of your office mates looking over at you a number of times during the past few days. At first she looked away quickly, but now she smiles every time you look up and catch her looking at you. You've been under a lot of pressure at work lately and have been extremely busy. You can't understand why she keeps looking at you. You've decided to ask.

_____

_____

_____

_____

3.4 PERCEPTION CHECKING

LEARNING OBJECTIVES

- Explain how the influences on perception listed in this chapter affect communication in a specific situation.
- Demonstrate how you might use the skill of perception checking in a significant relationship.

INSTRUCTIONS

1. Identify a situation in your life in which a perception check might be appropriate. Describe the situation to the person who will be evaluating your skill. Possible topics: controversial issues, things that "bug" you, perceived injustices, personal dilemmas, and misperceptions.
2. Deliver a complete perception check to your evaluator, without using notes, following the criteria listed in Chapter 3 of *Looking Out/Looking In* and outlined in the checklist below.

CHECKLIST

_____ Describes background for a potential perception-checking situation.

_____ Delivers complete perception check

      _____ Reports at least one behavior that describes, without evaluating or judging, what the person has said or done.

      _____ States two interpretations that are distinctly different, equally probable, and are based on the reported behavior.

      _____ Makes a sincere request for feedback clarifying how to interpret the reported behavior.

_____ Verbal and nonverbal behavior

      _____ Reflects sincere desire for clarification of the perception.

      _____ Sounds realistic and consistent with style of the speaker.

      _____ Uses nonthreatening, nondefensive voice and eye contact.

_____ Realistically and clearly assesses how perception checking and other alternatives can be used in everyday life.

      _____ In situation described here.

      _____ In other situations (be specific).

1. Describe how well perception checking might (or might not) work in the situation you have chosen. If you do not think a complete perception check is the best approach for this situation, explain why and describe a more promising alternative.

_____

_____

_____

_____

2. Describe various channels you can use for perception-checking.

_____

_____

_____

_____

3. What is the impact on the person using a perception check of having to think of more than one possible interpretation?

_____

_____

_____

_____

4. What is the impact on the person hearing the perception check of hearing more than one possible interpretation?

_____

_____

_____

_____

5. What would you predict are some long and short term effects on relationships in which people use more perception checks? Consider employee/employer, parent/child, co-workers, friends, and partners.

_____

_____

_____

_____

3.5 MEDIATED MESSAGES – PERCEPTION

LEARNING OBJECTIVES

- Describe how the processes of selection, organization, interpretation, and negotiation shape communication in a given situation.
- Explain how the influences on perception affect communication in a specific situation.

INSTRUCTIONS

Discuss each of the questions below in your group. Prepare written answers for your instructor, or be prepared to contribute to a large group discussion, comparing your experiences with those of others in your class.

1. Think of ways in which messages sent through mediated messages may contribute to misperceptions. (Example: I called my grandmother and she thought my tone of voice sounded like I was irritated with her; she didn't say anything to me at the time, but complained to my mother about me.)

_____

_____

_____

_____

2. How do the influences on perception (physiological or cultural differences, social roles, self-concept) affect these mediated misperceptions? (Example: Physiological: I was tired when I called my grandmother and I know she has age-related hearing problems.)

_____

_____

_____

_____

3. Prepare a perception-checking statement that could be used in a mediated context. Specify the mediated channel and the likelihood of success of the perception-checking attempt. (Example: "When you said in your last e-mail that you were busy on Saturday, I wondered if you had a previous commitment or if you were irritated with me for some reason I'm not aware of and so don't want to see me. What did you mean?" I think this perception-checking statement gives my partner a way to bring up anything that might be wrong, so it has a good likelihood of success.)

_____

_____

_____

_____

4. Are there times when using perception checks in mediated contexts might be preferable to using them face-to-face? Explain. Are there times when perception checks in mediated contexts might be less effective or appropriate? Explain.

_____

_____

_____

_____

3.6 PERCEPTION

LEARNING OBJECTIVES

- Explain how the influences on perception listed in this chapter affect communication in a specific situation.
- Analyze how the tendencies described in this chapter have distorted your perceptions of another person, and hence your communication. Use this information to present a more accurate alternative set of perceptions.
- Demonstrate how you might use the skill of perception checking in a significant relationship.

INSTRUCTIONS

Use the following case to explore the variety of communication issues involved in communication and perception.

CASE

Jorge is a registered nurse at a facility that cares for about 80 elderly patients. Jorge has been at the facility longer than any of the other nurses and has his choice of schedule; he believes he deserves this because of his service and seniority. There is now a shortage of nurses. Jorge's supervisor, Marisa, has been trying to hire new nurses, some of whom will only work if they can have Jorge's schedule. Marisa and Jorge are meeting to discuss the situation.

1. What factors are likely to influence the perceptions of Jorge and Marisa?

_____

_____

_____

_____

2. Prepare perception-checking statements for Jorge and Marisa to deliver to one another.

_____

_____

_____

_____

3.   How can Marisa and Jorge communicate competently in order to come to a constructive
      conclusion to this situation?

      _____

      _____

      _____

      _____

4.   What suggestions would you give Marisa and Jorge advice based on information in this
      chapter? Cite information from the text to back up your suggestions.

      _____

      _____

      _____

      _____

3.7 ASSESSING OUR PERCEPTION

LEARNING OBJECTIVES
- Explain how the influences on perception listed in this chapter affect communication in a specific situation.
- Analyze how the tendencies described on in the text have distorted your perceptions of another person, and hence your communication. Use this information to present a more accurate alternative set of perceptions.

INSTRUCTIONS: Predict the feelings of a classmate on a current issue such as politics, economy, or pop culture. List the issue below and then list the reason for your prediction.

Classmate # 1 Prediction:

_____

_____

_____

_____

Classmate # 2 Prediction:

_____

_____

_____

_____

Classmate #3 Prediction:

_____

_____

_____

_____

Now that you have predicted what your classmates might feel on a certain issue, ask them how they feel on this issue and record their responses below.

Classmate 1 Response:

_____

_____

_____

_____

Classmate 2 Response:

_____

_____

_____

_____

Classmate 3 Response:

_____

_____

_____

_____

Now compare your classmates' responses with your predictions. Were your predictions accurate? What made you make your initial predication about each of your classmates and how has your perception on them changed since doing this exercise?

Classmate # 1

_____

_____

_____

_____

Classmate # 2

_____

_____

_____

_____

Classmate # 3

_____

_____

_____

_____

STUDY GUIDE

CHECK YOUR UNDERSTANDING

TRUE/FALSE

Mark the statements below as true or false. Correct statements that are false on the lines below to create a true statement.

_____ 1. Androgynous males have a smaller repertoire of behaviors than masculine males.

_____

_____ 2. Selection, organization, interpretation, and negotiation comprise the steps of the perception process.

_____

_____ 3. The fact that we pay attention to some things and ignore others illustrates the fact that selection is an objective process.

_____

_____ 4. Allowing children to experience and manage frustrating events can help increase their empathic concern for others in later life.

_____

_____ 5. Generalizations and stereotypes of groups are generally accurate for everyone in the group.

_____

_____ 6. The halo effect is the tendency to form an overall positive impression of a person on the basis of one positive characteristic.

_____ 7. Adrenal and sex hormones affect the way both men and women relate to others.

_____

_____ 8. All cultures view talk as desirable, using it for social purposes as well as to perform tasks.

_____

_____ 9. Societal gender roles and stereotypes do not dramatically affect perception.

_____

_____ 10. The way we perceive ourselves influences our opinions of ourselves, but not our opinions of others.

_____

_____ 11. Since we are able to perceive with our senses, our perceptions make us aware of all that is going on around us.

_____

_____ 12. Culture plays an important role in our ability to understand the perspectives of others.

_____

_____ 13. Recent studies show that humans are "hard-wired" to empathize with one another.

_____

_____ 14. Cognitive complexity is the ability to construct one framework for a variety of issues.

_____

COMPLETION

Fill in the blanks below with the correct terms chosen from the list below.

narrative	self-serving bias	sympathy
the pillow method	empathy	stereotypes
punctuation	ethnocentrism	
androgynous	individualist culture	

1. _____ belief that one's culture is superior to others.

2. _____ is the determination of causes and effects in a series of interactions.

3. _____ is a story created by shared perspectives to explain events and behavior.

4. _____ is the tendency to judge ourselves in the most generous terms possible.

5. _____ is the ability to re-create another person's perspective.

6. _____ is one means for boosting empathy and cognitive complexity.

7. _____ are exaggerated generalizations associated with a categorizing system.

8. _____ is an example of a psychological sex type that influences perception.

9. _____ is feeling compassion for another person.

10. _____ is generally less adept at perspective-taking.

MULTIPLE CHOICE

RECOGNIZING PERCEPTION-CHECKING ELEMENTS

For each of the following statements, identify which element of the perception-checking statement is missing. Place the letter of the most accurate evaluation of the statement on the line before the statement.

a. This statement doesn't describe behavior.
b. This statement doesn't give two distinctly different interpretations.
c. This statement doesn't request clarification of the behavior in an open-ended way.
d. There is nothing missing from this perception-checking statement.

_____ 1. "Why did you send me those flowers? Is this a special occasion or what?"

_____ 2. "When you went straight to bed when you came home, I thought you were sick. Are you all right?"

_____ 3. "You must be either really excited about your grades or anxious to talk about something important. What's going on?"

_____ 4. "When you ran out smiling, I figured you were glad to see me and ready to go, or maybe you were having such a good time here you wanted to stay longer."

_____ 5. "I thought you were angry with me when you didn't come over this afternoon like you'd said you would. But then I thought maybe something came up at work. What is it?"

_____ 6. "When you told me you expected to get an outline with my report, I thought you were trying to trick me into doing more work, or maybe you didn't realize that wasn't part of my job."

_____ 7. "When you told everyone my parents own the company, you must have been indicating I was hired here only because of them. Is that what you think?"

_____ 8. "When you passed the ball to me, I thought you wanted me to shoot. Did you?"

_____ 9. "Why is it that you're so pleased with yourself? Did you win the lottery or accomplish something great? What's up?"

_____ 10. "Dad, when you told my friend Art what a great athlete you think I am, I thought you were either really proud of me and wanted to brag a little, or maybe you wanted to see what Art and I had in common by the way he responded. What were your intentions?"

CHAPTER 3 STUDY GUIDE ANSWERS

TRUE/FALSE

1. F		4. T		7. T		10. F		13. T
2. T		5. F		8. F		11. F		14. F
3. F		6. T		9. F		12. T		

COMPLETION

1. ethnocentrism
2. punctuation
3. narrative
4. self-serving bias
5. empathy
6. the pillow method
7. stereotypes
8. androgynous
9. sympathy
10. individualist cultures

MULTIPLE CHOICE

1. b		3. a		5. d		7. b, c		9. a
2. b, c		4. c		6. c		8. b		10. d

CHAPTER FOUR

Emotions: Feeling, Thinking, and Communicating

OUTLINE

Use this outline to take notes as you read the chapter in the text and/or as your instructor lectures in class.

I. **WHAT ARE EMOTIONS?**
   A. Physiological Factors
   B. Nonverbal Reactions
   C. Cognitive Interpretations
   D. Verbal Expression
	_____
	_____
	_____
	_____

II. **INFLUENCES ON EMOTIONAL EXPRESSION**
   A. Personality
   B. Culture
   C. Gender
   D. Social Conventions
   E. Fear of Self-Disclosure
   F. Emotional Contagion
	_____
	_____
	_____
	_____

III. **GUIDELINES FOR EXPRESSING EMOTIONS**
   A. Recognize Feelings
   B. Recognize the Difference between Feeling, Talking, and Acting
   C. Expand Your Emotional Vocabulary
      1. Avoid emotional counterfeits
        a. express verbally
	_____
	_____
	_____
	_____

88

        b. use single words

        c. describe what's happening to you

        d. describe what you'd like to do

    2. Avoid minimizing feelings

    3. Avoid coded feelings

    4. Focus on a specific set of circumstances

  D. Share Multiple Feelings

  E. Consider When and Where to Express your Feelings

  F. Responsibility for your Feelings

  G. Communication Channel

IV. MANAGING DIFFICULT EMOTIONS

  A. Facilitative and Debilitative Emotions

    1. Intensity

    2. Duration

  B. Sources of Debilitative Emotions

    1. Physiology

    2. Emotional memory

    3. Self-talk

  C. Irrational Thinking and Debilitative Emotions

    1. Fallacy of perfection

    2. Fallacy of approval

    3. Fallacy of shoulds

    4. Fallacy of overgeneralization

        a. limited amount of evidence

        b. exaggerated shortcomings

    5. Fallacy of causation

        a. belief: you cause emotions in others

        b. belief: others cause your emotions

    6. Fallacy of helplessness

    7. Fallacy of catastrophic expectations

D. Minimizing Debilitative Emotions 　1.　Monitor your emotional reactions 　2.　Note the activating event 　3.　Record your self-talk 　4.　Reappraise your irrational beliefs	

KEY TERMS

debilitative emotions

emotional contagion

emotional intelligence

emotion labor

facilitative emotions

fallacy of approval

fallacy of causation

fallacy of catastrophic expectations

fallacy of helplessness

fallacy of overgeneralization

fallacy of perfection

fallacy of shoulds

reappraisal

rumination

self-talk

ACTIVITIES

4.1 THE COMPONENTS OF EMOTION

LEARNING OBJECTIVES

- Describe how the four components listed in this chapter affect your emotions, and hence your communication in an important situation.

INSTRUCTIONS

1. Read the situations below and describe how the emotions you would experience might manifest themselves in each of the components listed. If you are working in a group, after all have finished, compare the responses of group members.
2. Next record three examples of your own (include the incident, physiological changes, nonverbal reactions, cognitive interpretations, and verbal expressions). If you wish, share one example with the group.

Example

Incident: _____

Physiological changes: _____

Nonverbal reactions: _____

Cognitive interpretations: _____

Verbal expression: _____

1. Incident: Your romantic partner says, "I need to talk to you about something."

    Physiological changes: _____

    Nonverbal reactions: _____

    Cognitive interpretations: _____

    Verbal expression: _____

91

2. Incident: You run into an "ex" while out with a new partner.

   Physiological changes: _____

   Nonverbal reactions: _____

   Cognitive interpretations: _____

   Verbal expression: _____

3. Incident: As you're telling a story, you notice your listener stifle a yawn.

   Physiological changes: _____

   Nonverbal reactions: _____

   Cognitive interpretations: _____

   Verbal expression: _____

4. Incident: Your professor says, "I'd like to see you in my office after class."

   Physiological changes: _____

   Nonverbal reactions: _____

   Cognitive interpretations: _____

   Verbal expression: _____

YOUR EXAMPLES

1. Incident: _____

   Physiological changes: _____

   Nonverbal reactions: _____

   Cognitive interpretations: _____

   Verbal expression: _____

2. Incident: _____

   Physiological changes: _____

   Nonverbal reactions: _____

   Cognitive interpretations: _____

   Verbal expression: _____

3. Incident: _____

   Physiological changes: _____

   Nonverbal reactions: _____

   Cognitive interpretations: _____

   Verbal expression: _____

93

4.2 EXPRESS THE FEELINGS

LEARNING OBJECTIVES

- Apply the guidelines for effectively communicating emotions in an important situation.

INSTRUCTIONS

I.   Analyze the statements below to determine which of the seven guidelines for expressing emotions are followed or ignored. There may be more than one.

   A. Recognize Feelings

   B. Recognize the Difference between Feeling, Talking, and Acting

   C. Expand Your Emotional Vocabulary

      1.   Avoid emotional counterfeits

      2.   Express verbally

        a. Use single words

        b. Describe what's happening to you

        c. Describe what you'd like to do

      3.   Avoid minimizing feelings

      4.   Avoid coded feelings

      5.   Focus on a specific set of circumstances

   D. Share Multiple Feelings

   E. Consider When and Where to Express Your Feelings

   F. Accept Responsibility for Your Feelings

   G. Be Mindful of the Communication Channel

II. Rewrite statements that do not follow the above guidelines to clearly or accurately express the speaker's feelings.

III. Record examples of your own at the end of the exercise.

EXAMPLE

That's the most disgusting thing I've ever heard!

Analysis: *This isn't a satisfactory statement, since the speaker isn't clearly claiming that he or she is*

disgusted. The speaker doesn't seem to recognize feelings (1) and doesn't verbally express a feeling(2-B) and doesn't accept responsibility by using "I" language (F).

Restatement: *I'm upset and angry that those parents left their young children alone overnight.*

___

1.   You're being awfully sensitive about that.

   Analysis _____

   Restatement _____

   _____

2. I can't figure out how to approach him.

   Analysis _____

   Restatement _____

   _____

3. I'm confused about what you want from me.

   Analysis _____

   Restatement _____

   _____

4. I feel as if you're trying to hurt me.

   Analysis _____

   Restatement _____

   _____

5. You make me so mad when you're late.

   Analysis _____

   Restatement _____

   _____

6. I'm sort of upset with your behavior and a little bit annoyed that you don't apologize.

   Analysis _____

   Restatement _____

   _____

7. I see you're all in there enjoying the game while I clean up the kitchen.

   Analysis _____

   Restatement _____

95

8. I feel like the rug's been pulled out from under me.

   Analysis _____

   Restatement _____

   _____

Now record three feeling statements of your own. Analyze and, if necessary, restate.

1. _____.

   Analysis _____

   Restatement _____

   _____

2. _____.

   Analysis _____

   Restatement _____

   _____

3. _____.

   Analysis _____

   Restatement _____

   _____

FEEDBACK TO "4.2 EXPRESS THE FEELINGS"

1. The speaker here is labeling another's feelings, but saying nothing about his or her own feelings. Is the speaker concerned, irritated, or indifferent? We don't know. Possible restate: "I worried that I teased you too much about your hair."
2. The emotion here is implied but not stated. The speaker might be frustrated, perplexed, or tired. Possible restate: "I'm nervous about telling him why I was absent."
3. Here is a clear statement of the speaker's emotional state.
4. The statement is emotionally counterfeit. Just because we say "I feel" doesn't mean a feeling is being expressed. This is an interpretation statement because "I feel" can be replaced by "I think." The speaker is expressing that "I think you tried to hurt me" and could then go on to state "I'm anxious about trusting you after you lied to me last week."

96

5. The speaker doesn't accept responsibility but blames the other person. Possibly there are multiple feelings. Possible restate: "I feel frustrated, hurt, and angry when you're late."
6. The use of minimizing words like "sort of" "a bit." Possible restate: "I'm upset with your behavior and annoyed that you don't apologize."
7. The statement is coded. Possible restate: "I feel used and taken for granted and would like some help cleaning up so we can all watch the game."
8. Here's a metaphorical statement of feeling, strongly suggesting surprise or shock. This sort of message probably does an adequate job of expressing the emotion here, but it might be too vague for some people to understand. Possible restate: "I feel insecure right now since I didn't get the job I was expecting."

4.3 STATING EMOTIONS EFFECTIVELY

LEARNING OBJECTIVES

- Describe how the four components listed in this chapter affect your emotions, and hence your communication in an important situation.
- Describe how the influences on emotional expression listed in this chapter have affected your communication in an important relationship.
- Apply the guidelines for effectively communicating emotions in an important situation.

INSTRUCTIONS

I. Identify what's ineffective or unclear about each of the following feeling statements.
II. Rewrite the feeling statements making them more effective using the guidelines from your text:
- A. Recognize Feelings
- B. Recognize the Difference between Feeling, Talking, and Acting
- C. Expand Your Emotional Vocabulary
  - 1. Avoid emotional counterfeits
  - 2. Express verbally
    - a. Use single words
    - b. Describe what's happening to you
    - c. Describe what you'd like to do
  - 3. Avoid minimizing feelings
  - 4. Avoid coded feelings
  - 5. Focus on a specific set of circumstances
- D. Share Multiple Feelings
- E. Consider When and Where to Express Your Feelings
- F. Accept Responsibility for Your Feelings
- G. Be Mindful of the Communication Channel

FEELING STATEMENT	IDENTIFY INEFFECTIVE, UNCLEAR ELEMENTS/REWRITE STATEMENT
EXAMPLE *When you complimented me in front of everyone at the party, I was really embarrassed.*	*I didn't express the mixed emotions I was feeling. I could have expressed this better by saying, "When you complimented me last night at the party, I was glad you were proud of me, but I was embarrassed that so many people heard it."*
1. You should be more sensitive.	

FEELING STATEMENT	IDENTIFY INEFFECTIVE, UNCLEAR ELEMENTS/REWRITE STATEMENT
2. I get kind of jealous when you have lunch with colleagues.	
3. I don't hear anyone offering to help with this project.	
4. Well, I guess you don't really care about this – or me.	
5. When you act like that, I don't want to be seen with you.	
6. You make me happy.	
7. Why should I help you now? You never show me any appreciation.	
8. I was a little ticked off when you didn't show up.	
9. You jerk—you forgot to put gas in the car!	
10. It's about time you paid up.	
11. I guess I'm a little attracted to him.	
12. With all that's happened, I feel like I'm in a time warp.	

99

4.4 EMOTIONAL LANGUAGE - SELF-TALK

LEARNING OBJECTIVES

- Identify and reappraise the fallacies that are creating debilitative emotions in an important situation. Explain how more rational thinking can lead to more constructive communication.

INSTRUCTIONS

1. In groups, analyze the statements below.
2. Expand the self-talk behind each statement by using details from your experience to help discover things people often say to themselves.
3. Identify any fallacies contained in the self-talk: approval, overgeneralization, perfection, helplessness, shoulds, catastrophic expectations, causation
4. Reappraise any irrational self-talk.
5. As a group, record the most common examples of your own self-talk, the fallacies involved, and the reappraising you need to do to keep emotionally healthy.

STATEMENT	SELF-TALK	FALLACIES	REAPPRAISE ANY FALLACIES
Example: *She's so critical.*	*She never has anything good to say. She drives me crazy. I can't stand her. I'll never be able to make her happy.*	*Overgeneralization, Causation, Helplessness, Approval*	*I need to focus on the good things she does say, not the criticisms. She doesn't make me crazy; I let her get to me. If I don't like what she is saying at the moment, I can leave. It would be nice to please her, but I don't need her approval to be happy.*
1. No one appreciates me around here.			
2. He's so moody.			

STATEMENT	SELF-TALK	FALLACIES	REAPPRAISE ANY FALLACIES
3. I don't know why I even bother to study for her stupid tests.			
4. Why can't he be more sensitive to my feelings?			
5. She is so embarrassing because she has no manners.			
6. He's a jerk just like his brother.			
7. She's the perfect boss. I'll be completely satisfied in this job.			
8. I'll never get out of here with all her talking.			

101

STATEMENT	SELF-TALK	FALLACIES	REAPPRAISE ANY FALLACIES
9. I can't believe you told me to buy this worthless car.			
10. It's no use talking to him; he's so unreasonable.			

YOUR OWN EXAMPLES: STATEMENT	SELF-TALK	FALLACIES	REAPPRAISE ANY FALLACIES
1.			
2.			
3.			
4.			

4.5 REAPPRAISING IRRATIONAL THOUGHTS

LEARNING OBJECTIVES

- Identify and reappraise the fallacies that are creating debilitative emotions in an important situation. Explain how more rational thinking can lead to more constructive communication.

INSTRUCTIONS

1. Use the chart provided to record activating events in which you experience communication-related debilitative emotions. The events needn't involve overwhelming, intense or intimae feelings; consider mildly debilitative emotions as well.
2. For each incident (activating event), record the self-talk that leads to the emotion you experienced.
3. If the self-talk you've identified is based on any of the irrational fallacies described in *Looking Out/Looking In*, identify them.
4. In each case where irrational thinking exists, reappraise the irrational fallacies and provide an alternative, more rational interpretation of the event.
5. After completing the examples, record your conclusions here (or put them on a separate page):

CONCLUSIONS

1. What are the situations in which you often experience debilitative emotions?

   _____

   _____

   _____

2. What irrational beliefs do you subscribe to most often? Label them and explain.

   _____

   _____

   _____

104

3. How can you think more rationally to reduce the number and intensity of debilitative emotions? (Give specific examples related to other aspects of your life, as well as referring to the activating events you have described in this exercise.)

_____

_____

_____

ACTIVATING EVENT	SELF-TALK	IRRATIONAL FALLACIES	EMOTION(S)	REAPPRAISE FALLACIES AND PROVIDE ALTERNATE RATIONAL THINKING
Example: *Getting ready for job interview*	*The employer will ask me questions I can't answer. I'll mess up for sure. I'll never get a good job—it's hopeless!*	*catastrophic failure overgeneralizati on helplessness*	*apprehension despair*	*I've prepared for the questions and the interview, so if I'm asked something I don't know, I'll say I'll get back to them on that. I have interpersonal skills. I'll find a good job with time and effort.*
1.				
2.				

ACTIVATING EVENT	SELF-TALK	IRRATIONAL FALLACIES	EMOTION(S)	REAPPRAISE FALLACIES AND PROVIDE ALTERNATE RATIONAL THINKING
3.				
4.				
5.				

4.6 MESSAGES – EXPRESSING EMOTION

LEARNING OBJECTIVES

- Describe how the influences on emotional expression listed in this chapter have affected your communication in an important relationship.
- Apply the guidelines for effectively communicating emotions in this chapter in an important situation.

INSTRUCTIONS

Discuss each of the questions below in your group. Prepare written answers for your instructor, or be prepared to contribute to a large group discussion, comparing your experiences with those of others in your class.

1. Describe how to recognize emotions communicated in mediated channels such as post-it notes, e-mail, and instant messaging.

_____

_____

_____

_____

2. Emotional expression may be more difficult in a mediated context (e.g., lack of touch or facial expression to communicate your empathy). On the other hand, mediated contexts may make emotional expression easier (e.g., write a note upon the death of someone rather than face them). Cite examples from your life where you used mediated contexts to express emotion.

_____

_____

_____

_____

3. In written communication, some stylistic devices (underlining, exclamation marks, capital letters, emoticons like the smiley, winking or sad face) indicate emotion. How effective do you think these can be in expressing emotion? How easily and how often are they understood? Misunderstood?

_____

_____

_____

_____

4. Compare and contrast the effectiveness of voice-messages and text-messages for conveying emotion through words.

_____

_____

_____

_____

4.7 EMOTIONS – REAPPRAISAL

LEARNING OBJECTIVES

- Identify and reappraise the fallacies that are creating debilitative emotions in an important situation. Explain how more rational thinking can lead to more constructive communication.
- Describe how the influences on emotional expression listed in the text have affected your communication in an important relationship.
- Apply the guidelines for effectively communicating emotions in an important situation.

INSTRUCTIONS

We all have emotionally charged events in our lives. Think back on three emotionally charged events in your life. Briefly describe the event in the space below. Then describe the emotions this event brings to mind and how you can use reappraisal to change the emotional impact of this event.

Event 1 _____

Emotions Felt:

_____

_____

Reappraisal:

_____

_____

Event 2 _____

Emotions Felt:

_____

_____

Reappraisal:

_____

_____

Event 3 _____

Emotions Felt:

_____

_____

Reappraisal:

_____

_____

4.8 ASSESSING NONVERBAL REACTIONS

LEARNING OBJECTIVES
- Apply the guidelines for effectively communicating emotions in an important situation.

INSTRUCTIONS: Watch a television program or a scene from a movie with the mute button on. Observe four nonverbal reactions and predict the possible emotional meaning behind them without listening to the verbal communication. Describe what you observed below and predict the possible nonverbal meaning below.

Observation 1

_____

_____

Possible Nonverbal Meaning

_____

_____

Observation 2

_____

_____

Possible Nonverbal Meaning

_____

_____

Observation 3

_____

_____

Possible Nonverbal Meaning

_____

_____

STUDY GUIDE

CHECK YOUR UNDERSTANDING

TRUE/FALSE

Mark the statements below as true or false. Correct statements that are false on the lines below to create a true statement.

_____ 1. Marriage researcher John Gottaman found that when couples are in such intense conflict that bodily changes occur (increase heart rate, a rise in blood pressure, a dilation of pupils) effective problem solving is impeded.

_____

_____ 2. Emotion labor refers to situations where managing and suppressing emotions is appropriate and necessary.

_____

_____ 3. While expression of emotion varies with culture and gender, scholars find that around the world both men and women consistently and similarly speak the phrase "I love you."

_____

_____ 4. In mainstream North American society, the unwritten rules of communication encourage the direct expression of most emotion.

_____

_____ 5. "I feel confined" is an emotional counterfeit statement.

_____

_____ 6. Using many words to express a feeling is better than just summarizing feelings in a few words.

_____

_____ 7. When thoughts are irrational, unwelcome emotions can interfere with effective communication.

_____

113

_____ 8. Reappraisal involves changing our thoughts to help manage our emotions.

_____

_____ 9. Subscribing to the myth of perfection usually enhances your own self-esteem, but it usually doesn't keep others from liking you.

_____

_____ 10. The fallacy of causation exists in two forms: you believe others cause your emotions or you believe you cause others' emotions.

_____

COMPLETION

Fill in the blanks below with the correct terms chosen from the list below.

catastrophic expectations   helplessness   causation
overgeneralization   shoulds   approval
perfection   activating event   reappraisal
rumination

1. _____ is an irrational fallacy that operates on the assumption that if something bad can possibly happen, it will.

2. _____ is an irrational fallacy that suggests that satisfaction in life is determined by forces beyond your control.

3. _____ is an irrational fallacy based on the belief that emotions are the result of other people and things rather than one's own self-talk.

4. _____ is an irrational fallacy that makes a broad claim based on a limited amount of evidence.

5. _____ is an irrational fallacy based on the inability to distinguish between what is and what ought to be.

6. _____ is an irrational fallacy in which people go to incredible lengths to seek acceptance from virtually everyone.

7. _____ is an irrational fallacy in which people believe that worthwhile communicators should be able to handle every situation with complete confidence and skill.

8. _____ is the single large incident or series of small incidents that lead to thoughts or beliefs about the incident.

114

9. _____ is the process of rethinking the meaning of emotionally charged events in a way that alter their emotional impact.

10. _____ is dwelling persistently on negative thoughts that, in turn, intensify negative feelings.

MULTIPLE CHOICE

Choose the letter of the irrational fallacy contained in the self-talk found below.

a. perfection
b. approval
c. shoulds
d. overgeneralization
e. causation
f. helplessness
g. catastrophic expectations

_____ 1. "If only I didn't put my foot in my mouth when I ask someone out."

_____ 2. "I just can't initiate conversations—that's all there is to it."

_____ 3. "He shouldn't be off with his friends on Friday night."

_____ 4. "If she doesn't like this shirt, I'll be so upset."

_____ 5. "There was a major fire the last time we left; there will probably be an earthquake this time."

_____ 6. "He's never romantic."

_____ 7. "She's always a cold fish; I'm lucky if I get a kiss."

_____ 8. "Other people ought to cut me some slack; they shouldn't be so critical."

_____ 9. "You're going to die or be seriously injured if you go to Mexico at spring break."

_____ 10. "I've had a class in interpersonal communication; I can't believe I insulted her just now."

_____ 11. "Shaw makes me so mad with all his great grades."

_____ 12. "She'll be devastated if I break up with her."

_____ 13. "It's not even worth trying to reach him."

_____ 14. "I hope they don't notice how much weight I've gained. They won't like it."

Choose the best answer for each of the statements below.

15. Which of the following statements about emotions and culture is true?
    a. The same events will generate the same emotions in all cultures.
    b. Some emotions seem to be experienced by people around the world.

115

    c. People from different cultures express happiness and sadness with different facial expressions.

    d. Fear of strangers is as strong in Japan as it is in the U.S.

16. Which of the following statements about rumination is not true?

    a. Rumination increases feelings of sadness.

    b. Rumination increases feelings of anxiety.

    c. Rumination increases feelings of depression.

    d. Rumination lessens aggression towards others.

17. Which of these represents coded emotions?

    a. I feel grateful when you bring soup to me when I'm sick.

    b. I'm upset because you borrowed my white-out.

    c. I feel like a door mat—just used by everyone.

    d. I don't hear any thank-you's. It sure would be nice to hear some appreciation.

18. Which of the following follows the text's guidelines for expressing feelings?

    a. "I feel like watching a movie."

    b. "I feel like you're lonely."

    c. "I'm irritated by the ticking clock."

    d. "I'm totally involved."

19. Which of the following *best* improves the expression of emotion in the statement "I feel like giving up"?

    a. "I'm frustrated after asking him to pay his telephone bill three times."

    b. "I'm going to kill him."

    c. "I am going to tell the landlord about this frustrating situation."

    d. "I feel he's been unreasonable."

20. In which job would emotion labor be needed the most?

    a. firefighter

    b. correctional officer

    c. judge

    d. emotion labor is equally important in all of these jobs

21. Which of the following statements about culture is true?

    a. All cultures are equal in every way.

    b. Emotions are lacking in most collectivistic cultures.

    c. People from different cultures express happiness and sadness with different facial expressions.

    d. The easiest way to understand a culture is to live within it for a period of time.

22. Which of the following statements about emotional intelligence is not true?

   a. Emotional intelligence is helpful in the workplace.
   b. Emotional intelligence is a sign of a competent communicator.
   c. Emotional intelligence is as important as cognitive intelligence.
   d. Emotional intelligence is a sign of an incompetent communicator.

CHAPTER 4 STUDY GUIDE ANSWERS

TRUE/FALSE

1. T	3. F	5. F	7. T	9. F
2. T	4. F	6. F	8. T	10. T

COMPLETION

1. catastrophic expectations	5. shoulds	9. reappraisal
2. helplessness	6. approval	10. rumination
3. causation	7. perfection	
4. overgeneralization	8. activating event	

MULTIPLE CHOICE

1. a	5. g	9. g	13. f	17. d
2. f	6. d	10. a	14. b	18. c
3. c	7. d	11. e	15. b	19. a
4. b	8. c	12. e	16. d	20. d
				21. d
				22. d

C H A P T E R   F I V E

Language: Barrier and Bridge

OUTLINE

Use this outline to take notes as you read the chapter in the text and/or as your instructor lectures in class.

I. **LANGUAGE IS SYMBOLIC**
   A. **Signs**
   B. **Symbols**

II. **UNDERSTANDINGS AND MISUNDERSTANDINGS**
   A. **Understanding Words: Semantic Rules**
     1. Equivocation
     2. Relative language
     3. Static evaluation
     4. Abstraction vs. behavioral language
       a. advantages
       b. problems
   B. **Understanding Structure: Syntactic Rules**
     1. Grammar
     2. Order
     3. Dialects
   C. **Understanding Context: Pragmatic Rules**
     1. Often unstated
     2. Relies on coordination
     3. Personal codes

118

III. THE IMPACT OF LANGUAGE

    A. Naming and Identity

        1. Personal identity

        2. Group identity

    B. Affiliation

        1. Convergence

        2. Divergence

    C. Power

        1. Powerless speech mannerism

        2. Culture and context

    D. Disruptive Language

        1. Fact-opinion confusion

        2. Fact-inference confusion

        3. Emotive language

    E. The Language of Responsibility

        1. "It" statements

        2. "But" statements

        3. "I" and "You" language

        4. "We" language

            a. "You" language judges

            b. "I" statements describe

                1) other's behavior

                2) your interpretation

                3) your feelings

                4) consequences of the behavior

            c. Advantages of "I" language

                1) accepts responsibility

                2) reduces defensiveness

                3) is more accurate

            d. Reservations about "I" language

                1) anger impedes use

                2) defensiveness with poor nonverbal

                3) sounds artificial without confidence

119

    4) too much sounds
     narcissistic
   e. "We" language
    1) may signal inclusion
     and commitment
    2) may speak improperly
     for others
    3) consider combining "I"
     and "we"

III. GENDER AND LANGUAGE

 A. Content

  1. Some common topics

  2. Sex talk restricted to same
   gender

  3. Many topics vary by gender

 B. Reasons for Communicating

  1. Build and maintain social
   relationships

   a. Men: more joking and good-
    natured teasing

   b. Women: more feelings and
    relationships

  2. Women—nourish relationships,
   build harmony

  3. Men – task-oriented, advice,
   status, independence

 C. Conversational Style

  1. Men: judge, direct, and "I"
   language

  2. Women: questions, intensifiers,
   emotion, uncertainty, support,
   maintain conversations

 D. Nongender Variables

  1. Occupation and social
   philosophy

  2. Historical and gender roles

V. CULTURE AND LANGUAGE
A. Verbal Communication Styles
1. Direct/indirect (low-context and high-context cultures)
2. Elaborate/succinct
3. Formality/informality
B. Language and World View
1. Linguistic relativism
2. Sapir-Whorf hypothesis

KEY TERMS

abstraction ladder

abstract language

behavioral language

"but" statements

convergence

divergence

emotive language

equivocal language

high-context cultures

"I" language

"it" statements

linguistic relativism

low-context cultures

powerless speech mannerisms

pragmatic rules

relative words

Sapir-Whorf hypothesis

semantic rules

static evaluation

syntactic rules

"we" language

"you" language

ACTIVITIES

5.1 MISUNDERSTOOD LANGUAGE

LEARNING OBJECTIVES

- Analyze a real or potential misunderstanding in terms of semantic or pragmatic rules.
- Construct a message at the optimal level of specificity or vagueness for a given situation.

INSTRUCTIONS

1. Label the language contained in each of the sentences below as relative language, static evaluation, or equivocal language.
2. Rewrite each sentence in more precise language.
3. Write your own examples of each variety of language in the spaces provided.

EXAMPLE 1
I'm trying to diet, so give me a **small** piece of cake.
Language: *Relative language*
Why you categorized it as you did and how can you best correct it: *It is relative because it can be compared to many other things; the best way to correct it is to use a number.*
Revised statement: *I'm trying to diet, so give me a piece of cake about two inches square.*

EXAMPLE 2
Helen **is** a troublemaker.
Language: *Static evaluation*
Why you categorized it as you did and how can you best correct it: *It is static because it uses the verb "to be" implying that troublemaker is a permanent condition of Helen. It can best be corrected with behavioral description.*
Revised statement: *Helen told my mother that I was out until 3 a.m. with Jim.*

EXAMPLE 3
There's a new book in the library; you should **check it out.**
Language: *Equivocal language*
Why you categorized it as you did and how can you best correct it: *It is equivocal because "check it out" can mean to appropriately remove it from the library in your name or to peruse it. Correct it by clarifying the meaning.*
Revised statement: *There's a new book in the library; you should peruse it and see if it is something you'd like to read.*

1. What do you want to know about our relationship?

   Language _____

Why you categorized it as you did and how can you best correct it: _____

_____

Revised statement _____

_____

2. They **are** real nerds.

Language _____

Why you categorized it as you did and how can you best correct it: _____

_____

Revised statement _____

_____

3. She's very **conservative**.

Language _____

Why you categorized it as you did and how can you best correct it: _____

_____

Revised statement _____

_____

4. I haven't done my laundry for a long time.

Language _____

Why you categorized it as you did and how can you best correct it: _____

_____

Revised statement _____

_____

5. Your essay should be brief.

   Language _____

   Why you categorized it as you did and how can you best correct it: _____

   _____

   Revised statement _____

   _____

6. My job isn't taking me anywhere.

   Language _____

   Why you categorized it as you did and how can you best correct it: _____

   _____

   Revised statement _____

   _____

   _____

7. She **is** such a braggart.

   Language _____

   Revised statement _____

   _____

8. You've got especially poor attendance.

   Language _____

   Why you categorized it as you did and how can you best correct it: _____

   _____

   Revised statement _____

   _____

Now write your own examples of each type of language and revise the statements to illustrate alternative language.

1. Equivocal language _____

   _____

   Revised _____

   _____

2. Relative language _____

   _____

   Revised _____

   _____

3. Static evaluation _____

   _____

   Revised _____

5.2 BEHAVIORAL LANGUAGE

LEARNING OBJECTIVES

- Construct a message at the optimal level of specificity or vagueness for a given situation.

INSTRUCTIONS

In each of the situations below, change the language to describe behavior in specific terms. Remember to focus on the <u>behavior</u> (e.g., Bev <u>did</u> "x," rather than Bev <u>is</u> "x"). If you are giving instructions, be specific enough (low abstractions) to clearly get your idea across to someone else.

EXAMPLE 1
John's a live wire.
John ran a 5K in the morning, volunteered for two hours at the homeless shelter in the afternoon, and then danced at a party until dawn.

EXAMPLE 2
Go over that way.
Go across the footbridge, turn right, go up the five large steps to the third building on your left.

1. Will you just wash the car the right way this time?

   _____

   _____

2. Natasha needs to get real.

   _____

   _____

3. You can't rely on Randy.

   _____

   _____

4. That teacher is hard-headed.

   _____

   _____

126

© 2014 Cengage Learning. All Rights Reserved. May not be copied, scanned, or duplicated, in whole or in part, except for use as permitted in a license distributed with a certain product or service or otherwise on a password-protected website for classroom use.

5. Get organized.

   _____

   _____

6. Josh just blows me off when I have something important to say.

   _____

   _____

7. He acts weird.

   _____

   _____

9. Do the report correctly this time.

   _____

   _____

10. My parents are understanding.

    _____

    _____

11. Get a decent movie this time.

    _____

    _____

12. I like it that your family is emotional.

    _____

    _____

5.3 EFFECTIVE LANGUAGE

LEARNING OBJECTIVES

- Analyze a real or potential misunderstanding in terms of semantic or pragmatic rules.
- Describe how principles presented in the section of this chapter titled "The Impact of Language" operate in your life.

INSTRUCTIONS

1. For each of the situations below, record the type of language used by the speaker. Evaluate its effectiveness. If you cannot identify with the situation, substitute one of your own.
2. Record the language you would use in response. Again, record your own situation and language if you have a relevant one.
3. Label the type of language used and evaluate its effectiveness. Focus on high and low abstraction, powerful or powerless speech mannerisms, facts or opinions, inferences, high- and low-context language styles and language and worldview.
4. Describe any alternative language you could use and its relative effectiveness.

EXAMPLE

Situation: Your supervisor at work has called you aside three times this week to correct work you have done. Each time she says, "You've messed up on this."

Type of language used with you/effectiveness: *My supervisor used "**you**" language and **high abstraction**. It wasn't very effective with me because I wasn't sure exactly what I'd messed up on, and I got very defensive, thinking she was about to fire me. She was very direct with me, however; she didn't keep*
*silent about what was bothering her (this is consistent with the **low-context culture** in which I live).*

Language you'd use in response: *"You're on me all the time about something or other."*

Type of language and effectiveness: *"**You**" language and **high abstraction**. This is probably not very*
effective. My supervisor is likely to get defensive. Actually, my supervisor may think this is "helpful" and
"caring" behavior and not realize that I am feeling hassled and threatened.

Alternative language: *"Ms. Gomez, I'm worried that I'm not doing my job correctly because you've*
corrected me three times this week. Which part of the report do you want corrected?" This "I"
language is more likely to let Ms. Gomez know what specifically is bothering me without raising a good deal of defensiveness. She's likely to appreciate my directness and specific request for help.

1. Situation: Your romantic partner has been extremely busy with school and work the last two weeks, and you've been feeling left out. When you suggest going out to a party, your partner replies, "You need a personal circus to have fun."
   Type of language used with you/effectiveness:

   _____

   _____

   Language you'd use in response:

   _____

   _____

   Type of language and effectiveness:

   _____

   _____

   Alternative language:

   _____

   _____

2. Situation: You have a hard time saying "no." Lately your roommate has been asking you to do chores that are not your responsibility. Tonight the roommate says, "You're such a great roommate. You won't mind doing the dishes for me tonight since I've got a date and you're just staying home anyway, will you?"
   Type of language used with you/effectiveness:

   _____

   _____

   Language you'd use in response:

   _____

   _____

Type of language and effectiveness:

_____

_____

Alternative language:

_____

_____

3. Situation: Cousins of yours are moving to town. They just called, addressing you by your old family nickname and said, "You lucky person, you get to have the pleasure of our company for a while until we find a place to live. We thought you'd be glad to have us." Type of language used with you/effectiveness:

_____

_____

Language you'd use in response:

_____

_____

Type of language and effectiveness:

_____

_____

Alternative language:

_____

_____

4. Situation: You're working on a project with a partner from class, and the partner says, "We'll never get this done. You're too meticulous about everything."
    Type of language used with you/effectiveness:

    _____

    _____

    Language you'd use in response:

    _____

    _____

    Type of language and effectiveness:

    _____

    _____

    Alternative language:

    _____

    _____

5. Situation: Your boss's five-year-old is visiting the workplace. The child has broken two items and is now running from door to door, laughing loudly. Two customers look your way. Your boss says, "Isn't he great? Really an energetic kid!"
    Type of language used with you/effectiveness:

    _____

    _____

    Language you'd use:

    _____

    _____

Type of language and effectiveness:

_____

_____

Alternative language:

_____

_____

Record a situation of your own here:

6. Situation:

_____

_____

Type of language used with you/effectiveness:

_____

_____

Language you'd use in response:

_____

_____

Type of language and effectiveness:

_____

_____

Alternative language:

_____

_____

132

5.4 MEDIATED MESSAGES--LANGUAGE

LEARNING OBJECTIVES

- Analyze a real or potential misunderstanding in terms of semantic or pragmatic rules.
- Describe how principles presented in the section of this chapter titled "The Impact of Language" operate in your life.
- In a given situation, analyze how gender and/or cultural differences may affect the quality of interaction.

INSTRUCTIONS

Discuss each of the questions below in your group. Prepare written answers for your instructor, or be prepared to contribute to a large group discussion, comparing your experiences with those of others in your class.

1. Our identity is tied to the names we use. Discuss your identity goals with the name(s) you use in mediated contexts (e.g., *your e-mail address, web site identities or your chat room identity*).

   _____

   _____

2. The language used in an answering machine, voice mail, or e-mail can be very businesslike or very informal. Discuss the pros and cons of formal versus informal mediated messages.

   _____

   _____

3. Sometimes people fail to adapt their language style to the medium they are using (e.g., *they leave a 5-minute voice mail that should have been summarized in 30 seconds*). Should different mediated channels contain more language or less? Specify two different mediated channels and how much language is appropriate for each.

   _____

   _____

4. Describe the gender or social role differences you have noticed in the <u>language</u> of mediated communication. (Example: *My son is more comfortable "talking" about emotions in e-mail, my daughter prefers the telephone.* Example: *My spouse's executive assistant uses very informal language to address me in an e-mail that is never used with me face-to-face.*)

   _____

   _____

5.5 LANGUAGE

LEARNING OBJECTIVES

- In a given situation, analyze how gender and/or cultural differences may affect the quality of interaction.
- Construct a message at the optimal level of specificity or vagueness for a given situation.
- Recast "you" statements into "I" or "we" statements to reflect your responsibility for the content of messages.

INSTRUCTIONS

Use the case below and the discussion questions that follow to discuss the variety of communication issues involved in effective communication. Make notes on this page, add other pages on your own, or prepare a group report/analysis based on your discussion. Add your own experiences to individualize the analysis.

CASE

Professor Polle paired Matt and Magda as class project partners. After three weeks both Matt and Magda came to their professor to complain about the other. Matt called Magda a "flake" and said she didn't work hard enough and didn't take the project seriously. Magda said that Matt was "arrogant," wanted the project done only her way, and didn't care about all the commitments Magda had. It was too late in the semester for the professor to give them new partners.

1. Identify the language that Matt and Magda are using about one another. What effect does using this language have on their perception of each other? On the successful completion of their project?

_____

_____

2. Rewrite the high level abstractions that Matt and Magda use with specific, concrete language. How could this change their perceptions? Improve their situation?

_____

_____

3. Give an example of an "I" language statement from any of the three persons that could improve the situation.

_____

_____

4. Gender and culture may influence the way language is used. Identify differences mentioned in your text and describe how those differences might apply to this situation.

_____

_____

STUDY GUIDE

CHECK YOUR UNDERSTANDING

TRUE/FALSE

Mark the statements below as true or false. For statements that are false, correct them on the lines below to create a true statement.

_____ 1. Words are not arbitrary symbols; they have meaning in and of themselves.

_____

_____ 2. Language can both *shape* our perceptions of the world and *reflect* our attitudes towards others.

_____

_____ 3. Since research shows that people are rated as more competent when their talk is free of powerless speech mannerisms, it is obvious that a consistently powerful style of speaking is always the best approach.

_____

_____ 4. Even in low context cultures there are times when indirect speech can help communicators achieve sound goals in ethically sound ways.

_____

_____ 5. Linguistics believe that we should view varying syntactic rules as deficient forms of English.

_____

_____ 6. "How are we feeling today?" is an example of "we" language.

_____

_____ 7. Naming children can be a way to express personal and ethnic identity.

_____

_____ 8. Women's behavior in conversations vary dramatically from men's behavior.

_____

136

_____ 9. Swearing patterns of bosses and coworkers can help people feel connected on the job.

_____

_____ 10. Men are more likely to use language to accomplish a job, while women are more likely to use language to nourish relationships.

_____

COMPLETION

Fill in the blanks below with the correct terms chosen from the list below.

abstraction ladder	equivocation	convergence	divergence	polite forms
tag questions	elaborateness	hedges	disclaimers	succinctness
formality	informality			

1. _____ is the process of adapting one's speech style to match that of others with whom the communicator wants to identify.

2. _____ in language use involve denying direct responsibility for the statement, such as "I could be wrong, but . . . "

3. _____ of language involve using respectful terms of address, such as "You're welcome, ma'am."

4. _____ involves speaking in a way that emphasizes a person's differences from the other persons with whom he or she is speaking .

5. _____ in language use involves using words that more than one commonly accepted definition, such as "They eat _healthy_ food."

6. _____ in language use involve a negation statement, such as "_Didn't you think_ that party was boring?"

7. _____ in language use make less of the feeling or intention statement, such as "I'm _rather_ upset."

8. _____ is an illustration of how the same phenomenon can be described at various levels of specificity.

9. _____ involves speaking with few words, and it is usually most extreme in cultures where silence is valued.

10. _____ involves speaking with rich and expressive terms, sometimes involving strong assertions and exaggerations.

11. _____ is a way of using correct grammar as a way of defining social position in some cultures.

12. _____ is a way of using language that is casually friendly and does not reflect a series of relational hierarchies in a particular culture.

MULTIPLE CHOICE

Label the examples of language given below by writing the letter of the language type illustrated on the line in front of the example.

a. inference   b. relative word   c. abstract words
d. emotive word   e. equivocal language

_____ 1. John didn't call so he must be angry.

_____ 2. I have a stomach problem.

_____ 3. That place is expensive.

_____ 4. That guy is a real hunk.

_____ 5. My car is hot. (Temperature inside? Overheating? Good-looking? Stolen?)

_____ 6. She left the meeting early; she must have been irritated.

_____ 7. When I said I'd always help bail you out, I didn't mean from jail, just that I'd help you pay your bills.

_____ 8. As your governor, I'd improve education in the state.

_____ 9. He showed up, so he must agree with the protest.

_____ 10. He's a real tight-wad.

_____ 11. All of the measures I've supported in Congress promote security.

_____ 12. Ian gave a long speech.

_____ 13. My grandfather is young.

_____ 14. My sister is a pill.

Choose the letter of the *least* abstract alternative to the high abstraction terms.

_____ 15. Jo's constantly complaining.

    a. Jo whines a lot.
    b. Jo complains often about the workload.
    c. Jo told me three times this week that she feels overworked.
    d. Every time we meet, Jo complains about all the work she does.

138

_____ 16. He can never do anything because he's always busy.

    a. He couldn't take me to dinner last night because he had to work.
    b. He can never do anything fun because he's always working.
    c. He didn't ever take time off to be with me.
    d. He works too much so we have a boring life.

_____ 17. There are a lot of problems associated with freedom.

    a. Freedom carries with it responsibility.
    b. Since I moved into my own apartment, I have to pay ten bills.
    c. I don't like all the responsibility of living on my own.
    d. My economic responsibilities limit my freedom.

_____ 18. Shannon is worthless as a roommate.

    a. Shannon is always gone, so she's really not part of our house.
    b. Shannon never does her part around here.
    c. Shannon's jobs seldom get done around here.
    d. Shannon has attended only one of our six house meetings.

_____ 19. Carlos is the most wonderful friend.

    a. Carlos has never told anyone about my fear of failing.
    b. Carlos listens to me about everything.
    c. Carlos is the best listener I've ever met.
    d. I can trust Carlos implicitly with all my secrets.

_____ 20. Keiko goes overboard in trying to make people like her.

    a. Keiko gave everyone on the team a valentine.
    b. Keiko is the biggest kiss-up you ever met.
    c. I think Keiko is trying to make my friends like her better than me.
    d. I want Keiko to stop trying to outdo everybody else.

Choose the best answer for each of the statements below:

_____ 21. Semantic misunderstandings arise when
    a. people assign the same meanings to the same words.
    b. people assign different meanings to different words.
    c. people assign different meanings to the same words.
    d. people assign the same meaning to different words.

_____ 22. One way to make words more measurable is to
   a. use words such as "doubtful, toss-up, likely, probable, good chance, and unlikely."
   b. use abstract concepts.
   c. use equivocal language.
   d. turn them into numbers.

_____ 23. One way to make words more effective to the listener is to
   a. use words that offend but get your point across.
   b. use abstract concepts.
   c. use equivocal language.
   d. adapt to the listeners language patterns.

_____ 24. Words are
   a. useless and should be avoided.
   b. arbitrary and their meaning is assigned by the receiver.
   c. the most important part of communication.
   d. helpful only if you chose the right ones.

CHAPTER 5 STUDY GUIDE ANSWERS

TRUE/FALSE

1. F	3. F	5. F	7. T	9. T
2. T	4. T	6. F	8. F	10. T

COMPLETION

1. convergence	5. equivocation	9. succinctness
2. disclaimers	6. tag questions	10. elaborateness
3. polite forms	7. hedges	11. formality
4. divergence	8. abstraction ladder	12. informality

MULTIPLE CHOICE

1. a	5. e	9. a	13. b	17. b	21. c
2. c	6. a	10. d	14. d	18. d	22. d
3. b	7. e	11. c	15. c	19. a	23. d
4. d	8. c	12. b	16. a	20. a	24. b

CHAPTER SIX

Nonverbal Communication: Messages Beyond Words

OUTLINE

Use this outline to take notes as you read the chapter in the text and/or as your instructor lectures in class.

I. **CHARACTERISTICS OF NONVERBAL COMMUNICATION**
   A. **Nonverbal Skills Are Vital**
   B. **All Behavior Has Communicative Value**
      1. Deliberate
      2. Unintentional
   C. **Nonverbal Communication Is Primarily Relational**
      1. Managing identity
      2. Defining relationships
      3. Conveying emotion
   D. **Nonverbal Communication Serves Many Functions**
      1. Repeating
      2. Complementing
      3. Substituting
      4. Accenting
      5. Regulating
      6. Contradicting
   E. **Nonverbal Communication Offers Deception Clues**

1. Leakage
2. Deception detection 101
   a. we are only accurate half the time.
   b. we overestimate our ability to detect other's lies.
   c. we have a strong tendency to judge other's messages as truthful.

F. **Nonverbal Communication Is Ambiguous**
   1. Silence
   2. Sexual behavior
   3. NVLD

II. INFLUENCES ON NONVERBAL COMMUNICATION

A. **Gender**
   1. Physical and social
   2. Cultural norms

B. **Culture**
   1. Sending nonverbal messages
   2. Interpreting nonverbal communication

III. TYPES OF NONVERBAL COMMUNICATION

A. **Body Movement**
   1. Body orientation
      a. Facing toward or away
      b. Signals interest or exclusion
   2. Posture
      a. Emotions
      b. Tension/relaxation
   3. Gestures
      a. Illustrators
      b. Emblems
      c. Adaptors (manipulators)
   4. Face and eyes

a. Face: number, speed, microexpressions

b. Eyes: involvement, attitude, dominance, interest

B. Voice (Paralanguage)

1. Emphasis

2. Tone, rate, pitch, volume, pauses (unintentional and vocalized)

3. Sarcasm

4. Credibility and liking

C. Touch (Haptics)

1. Signals type of relationship

2. Context matters: who, where, when

3. Shapes responses: liking

4. Essential to development and health

D. Appearance

1. Physical attractiveness

2. Clothing

E. Physical Space (proxemics)

1. Distance

   a. intimate

   b. personal

   c. social

   d. public

2. Territoriality

F. Physical Environment

1. Architecture and design

2. Shaping interactions

G. Time (Chronemics)

1. Status

2. Culture: monochromic/polychronic

KEY TERMS

accenting

adaptors

body orientation

chronemics

complementing

contradicting

emblems

gestures

haptics

illustrators

intimate distance

kinesics

leakage

manipulators

microexpression

mixed message

monochronic

nonverbal communication

paralanguage

personal distance

polychronic

posture

proxemics

public distance

regulating

repeating

social distance

substituting

territory

ACTIVITIES

6.1 DESCRIBING NONVERBAL STATES

LEARNING OBJECTIVES

- Explain the defining characteristics of nonverbal communication as described in this chapter.
- List and offer examples of each type of nonverbal message introduced in this chapter.
- Share appropriately your interpretation of another's nonverbal behavior with that person.

INSTRUCTIONS

1. For each of the statements below, record the nonverbal behaviors that reflect the attitude or emotions described.

2. Compare your responses with those of others in the class and note the similarities and differences in your responses.

3. For each item, describe on as many types of nonverbal behavior as you can: body movement (orientation, posture, gestures, face/eyes), voice, touch, appearance, physical space, physical environment, time.

EXAMPLE 1

He says I'm too eager to please.
I respond quickly after a request. I lean toward the person a lot. I smile and keep the smile on my face continuously. I gesture quickly. I stand a bit bowed over. I tilt my head to the side submissively.

EXAMPLE 2

She listens well.
Turns body toward me, leans forward, smiles once or twice, nods, maintains eye contact about 80 percent of the time.

  1. My boss is mean.

    _____

    _____

2. My co-workers say I don't treat them well.

_____

_____

3. He's not into this project.

_____

_____

4. She can't stop flirting.

_____

_____

5. They tell me I'm too tense.

_____

_____

6. She acts like she's in charge.

_____

_____

7. He makes a big deal of everything.

_____

_____

8. You need to act more sure of yourself.

_____

_____

9. He seems friendly.

_____

146

10. You're not exactly a ray of sunshine.

_____

_____

11. They tell me I'm too aggressive.

_____

_____

12. She's "hyper."

_____

_____

List how at least two of the preceding statements could be taken in both positive and negative ways (*i.e., number 6 could be positive if you are grateful that she's organizing things, but negative if you're resentful of her influence*).

_____

_____

_____

_____

List the nonverbal behaviors that are associated with the alternate interpretation (the one you didn't record initially) and your reaction. (*i.e., I can see the positive side of taking charge— assigning seating, standing erect, firm voice, keeping to a time schedule, nodding and making eye contact with those who should speak to you. There's often a small difference between the nonverbal behaviors I find positive and those I find annoying or bossy*).

_____

_____

_____

_____

6.2 DESCRIBING NONVERBAL BEHAVIORS

LEARNING OBJECTIVES

- Explain the defining characteristics of nonverbal communication as described in the text
- In a given situation, recognize your own nonverbal behavior and its relational significance.
- Monitor and manage your nonverbal cues in ways that achieve your goals.

INSTRUCTIONS

1. For each of the social situations below, list the nonverbal behaviors you believe will achieve the stated goal.
2. Compare your answers with those of others in your class.
3. Reflect on the behavior of yourself and others important to you. How might you change some of the nonverbal cues you display to communicate what you desire more effectively?
4. Use as many categories of nonverbal behavior as you can: Body movement (orientation, posture, gestures, face/eyes), voice, touch, appearance, physical space, physical environment, time.

Example:

Initiate conversation with a stranger at a party.

Make eye contact, offer hand in greeting, smile, come within four feet of other person, turn body toward other person, nod occasionally when other is talking.

1. Take control or exercise leadership in a class group.

_____

_____

2. Come across well in a job interview.

_____

_____

3. Tell an interesting joke or story.

_____

_____

4. Appear friendly and warm without "coming on too strong."

_____

_____

5. Signal your desire to leave a conversation when the other person keeps on talking.

_____

_____

6. Appear confident when asking boss for a raise.

_____

_____

7. Appear interested in class lecture.

_____

_____

8. Avoid talking with a person on a plane or bus.

_____

_____

9. Show kindness toward an elderly relative.

_____

_____

10. Appear concerned about a friend's dilemma.

_____

_____

149

11.   Describe two of your usual nonverbal behaviors in a particular context that you might want to change.

_____

_____

_____

_____

_____

12.   Why might you want to change them?

_____

_____

_____

_____

6.3 AMBIGUITY, CONTRADICTION, AND CONGRUENCE

LEARNING OBJECTIVES

- In a given situation, recognize your own nonverbal behavior and its relational significance.
- Monitor and manage your nonverbal cues in ways that achieve your goals.

INSTRUCTIONS

1. In each of the following situations, describe verbal and nonverbal behaviors likely to occur: body movement (orientation, posture, gestures, face/eyes), voice, touch, appearance, physical space, physical environment, time. Nonverbal behaviors seldom occur alone, so describe clusters of at least 3 nonverbal behaviors for each situation. Note whether the verbal and nonverbal behaviors are ambiguous, contradictory, or congruent. Finally, evaluate the possible consequences of the ambiguity, contradictions, or congruency.
2. Next describe situations from your own life and how you would send verbal and nonverbal messages. Include the possible consequences of your congruent or ambiguous behaviors.
3. After you've completed the examples, answer the questions about congruency/ambiguity.

SITUATION	YOUR VERBAL BEHAVIOR	YOUR NONVERBAL BEHAVIOR (USE A **CLUSTER** OF BEHAVIORS HERE)	ARE BEHAVIORS, CONTRADICTORY, AMBIGUOUS, OR CONGRUENT?	POSSIBLE CONSEQUENCES
EXAMPLE *Person I like a lot takes me out to dinner and I have a good time and enjoy the food.*	*"I'm really enjoying this; the food is terrific and so is the company."*	*I look at my partner when I talk, smiling and tilting my head, and leaning slightly forward. I touch my partner light on the arm and hand.*	*My verbal and nonverbal behaviors are congruent, not ambiguous.*	*I hope my partner will understand how much I care and enjoy our time together. I run the risk of being hurt if my partner's feelings don't match mine, but I'm willing to take that risk.*

SITUATION	YOUR VERBAL BEHAVIOR	YOUR NONVERBAL BEHAVIOR (USE A CLUSTER OF BEHAVIORS HERE)	ARE THE BEHAVIORS AMBIGUOUS?	POSSIBLE CONSEQUENCES
1. My boss asks me to work late when I've made other plans.				
2. My roommate asks, while I'm doing homework, if I can make dinner.				
3. My relative drops in to visit me when other people are over for the evening.				
4. My romantic partner says I act like I'm indifferent when we discuss our future.				
5. Our waiter starts to take my plate and asks if I'm finished while food is still on my plate.				

152

6. (your example)				
7. (your example)				
8. (your example)				

Reflections

1. Are there situations in which it is advantageous to express yourself ambiguously? Explain how sending one message verbally and another one nonverbally could be beneficial or explain why you believe it never is advantageous.

_____

_____

_____

_____

2. Describe situations in which ambiguity clearly is not desirable. Describe how you could best match your verbal and nonverbal behaviors in these situations.

_____

_____

_____

_____

_____

3. What are the ethical considerations of nonverbal ambiguity or contradiction? Is it ever ethical to intentionally be ambiguous or contradictory? Why or why not? Can you think of situations in which it is never or ever ethical to intentionally send ambiguous or contradictory nonverbal messages?

_____

_____

_____

_____

4. Are there situations in which nonverbal ambiguity or contradiction is unintentional and unavoidable? Explain your answer

_____

_____

_____

_____

6.4 NONVERBAL ANALYSIS

LEARNING OBJECTIVES

- Explain the defining characteristics of nonverbal communication as described in the text.

- Share appropriately your interpretation of another's nonverbal behavior with that person.

INSTRUCTIONS

Use the case below and the discussion questions that follow to discuss the variety of communication issues involved in effective communication. Make notes on this page, add other pages on your own, or prepare a group report/analysis based on your discussion. Add your own experiences to individualize the analysis.

CASE

Malena and Dolly are coworkers in different departments in a large company. Over coffee one day Malena tells Dolly that she's been feeling very uneasy lately about her boss's behavior. "I'm not exactly sure how to describe it," Malena says, "but I think he's coming on to me, and I don't know what to do."

1.   Malena would do well to be able to describe her boss's behavior. Imagine a situation like this and describe the possible behavior of Malena's boss.

_____

_____

2.   Which of the behavior's listed in question 1 might be intentional and which might be unintentional? Why?

_____

_____

3.   Describe possible intentional or unintentional nonverbal behaviors of Malena that might be misunderstood.

_____

_____

4. Using ideas from this and the previous chapters in the text, what could Malena do verbally and nonverbally to handle this issue?

_____

_____

_____

_____

6.5 ASSESSING NONVERBAL BEHAVIOR

LEARNING OBJECTIVES

- List and offer examples of each type of nonverbal message introduced in this chapter.

INSTRUCTIONS: Watch a scene in a movie or TV show on mute. Evaluate how the actor/actress uses nonverbal behavior to convey an emotion. Record your descriptions in the spaces below.

Scene 1_____

Emotion being conveyed_____

Body movement_____

Posture_____

Gestures_____

Face and eyes_____

Appearance_____

Scene 2_____

Emotion being conveyed_____

Body movement_____

Posture_____

Gestures_____

Face and Eyes_____

Appearance_____

STUDY GUIDE

CHECK YOUR UNDERSTANDING

TRUE/FALSE

Mark the statements below as true or false. Correct statements that are false on the lines below to create a true statement.

_____ 1. Nonverbal behaviors are, by their nature, intentional.

_____

_____ 2. Nonverbal communication encompasses abstract factors such as physical appearance, the environment in which we communicate, and the way we use time.

_____

_____ 3. The concept of nonverbal convergence illustrates that skilled communicators can adapt their behavior when interacting with members of other cultures or co-cultures in order to make the exchange more effective.

_____

_____ 4. Nonverbal communication is much better suited to expressing attitudes and feelings than it is to expressing concrete ideas.

_____

_____ 5. Research on nonverbal communication and lying shows that individuals who are trying to deceive others are less likely to show nonverbal evidence of lying if they haven't had a chance to rehearse their lying and when they feel strongly about the information being hidden.

_____

_____ 6. In studies of detecting lying, men are consistently more accurate than women at detecting the lies and discovering the underlying truth.

_____

_____ 7. Pupil dilation is less reliable than facial expressions in picking up on deception clues.

_____

_____ 8. Unlike verbal communication that is intermittent (starts and stops), nonverbal communication is continuous and never ending.

_____

159

_____ 9. The nonverbal impact of messages is more powerful than the verbal impact.

_____

_____ 10. Nonverbal communication is clearer than verbal communication.

_____

_____ 11. The concept of leakage is most often associated with deception.

_____

_____ 12. We are accurate in detecting deception only slightly more than half the time.

_____

_____ 13. Behaviors that have one meaning for members of the same culture or co-culture can be interpreted differently by members of another group.

_____

_____ 14. Women are more likely to believe the deception of an intimate partner than are men.

_____

_____ 15. When you use nonverbal behavior to regulate other's behavior, it guarantees that the other will pay attention to, interpret, or respond as you intended.

_____

COMPLETION

Fill in the blanks below with the correct terms chosen from the list below.

illustrator	intimate	personal	social	body orientation
relaxation	paralanguage	emblem	adaptor	touch
public	text-based messages			

1. _____ is the distance zone identified by Hall that ranges from four to about twelve feet; within it are the kinds of communication that usually occur in business.

2. _____ is a postural cue such as leaning back or lowering shoulders that a higher status person usually exhibits when not feeling threatened.

3. _____ is a deliberate, nonverbal behavior that has a very precise meaning known to virtually everyone within a cultural group.

4. _____ is the distance zone identified by Hall that ranges from eighteen inches to four feet and includes behavior found in most social conversations.

5. _____ is a gesture that accompanies speech but doesn't stand on its own.

6. _____ is the degree to which we face toward or away from someone with our body, feet, and head.

7. _____ is the distance zone identified by Hall that ranges from skin contact to about eighteen inches; we usually use this distance with people in private who are emotionally very close to us.

8. _____ is the distance zone identified by Hall that ranges from twelve feet outward and includes communication such as that found in a typical classroom.

9. _____ is nonverbal behavior that includes having a foreign accent.

10. _____ is nonverbal behavior that includes brushing up against someone.

11. _____ is an unconscious body movement that helps us adjust to the environment.

12. _____ can use linguistic shortcuts and acronyms to indicate nonverbal messages.

MULTIPLE CHOICE

Choose the letter of the type of nonverbal communication that is illustrated below.

a. environnent   b. paralinguistics   c. proxemics   d. territoriality

_____   1. No one dared to sit in Ralph's chair.

_____   2. Jeremy put a "NO ENTRANCE" sign on his door.

_____   3. The students rearranged the chairs in the classroom.

_____   4. Manuela stepped back three feet from her friend.

_____   5. The lovers were sitting only inches apart.

_____   6. Rob's voice softened when he spoke to her.

_____   7. There was a long pause after the decision was made.

_____   8. Mitchell sighed audibly.

_____   9. Gretchen took the third seat down from Yayoi.

_____   10. Kevin was annoyed that someone was leaning on his car.

a. body orientation   b. gesture   c. touch   d. face and eyes

_____   11. The children playfully kicked one another.

_____ 12. Professor Jimenez illustrated her lecture with many arm movements.

_____ 13. Leland shifted his shoulders toward the speaker.

_____ 14. Ernie avoided looking at her.

_____ 15. The executive stared at her employee.

_____ 16. Martin turned his body away from his brother.

_____ 17. The officer pointed in the correct direction.

_____ 18. Letoya didn't appreciate the slap on the back.

_____ 19. Blake set his jaw in disgust.

_____ 20. Francesca signaled "OK" across the room.

Choose the best answer for each of the statements below:

_____ 21. Paralanguage describes
   a. nonverbal, silent messages.
   b. vocal messages.
   c. verbal messages.
   d. nonverbal, vocal messages.

_____ 22. According to researchers women tend to
   a. smile less than men.
   b. use more facial expressions.
   c. use less facial expressions.
   d. are less vocally expressive than men.

_____ 23. Deceivers try to maintain a
   a. poker face when communicating.
   b. blank face when communicating.
   c. plain face when communicating.
   d. pleasant face when communicating.

_____ 24. Touch can
   a. increase liking.
   b. increase compliance.
   c. both a and b
   d. none of the above

CHAPTER 6 STUDY GUIDE ANSWERS

TRUE/FALSE

1. F	4. T	7. F	10. F	13. T
2. T	5. F	8. T	11. T	14. T
3. T	6. F	9. T	12. T	15. F

COMPLETION

1. social	5. illustrator	9. paralanguage
2. relaxation	6. body orientation	10. touch
3. emblem	7. intimate	11. adaptor
4. personal	8. public	12. text-based messages

MULTIPLE CHOICE

1. d	5. c	9. c	13. a	17. b	21. d
2. d	6. b	10. d	14. d	18. c	22. b
3. a	7. b	11. c	15. d	19. d	23. a
4. c	8. b	12. b	16. a	20. b	24. c

CHAPTER SEVEN

Listening: More Than Meets the Ear

OUTLINE

Use this outline to take notes as you read the chapter in the text or as your instructor lectures in class.

I. **LISTENING DEFINED**
   A. **Hearing vs. Listening**
   B. **Mindless Listening**
   C. **Mindful Listening**

II. **ELEMENTS IN THE LISTENING PROCESS**
   A. **Hearing**
   B. **Attending**
   C. **Understanding**
   D. **Responding**
   E. **Remembering**

III. **THE CHALLENGE OF LISTENING**
   A. **Types of Ineffective Listening**
      1. Pseudolistening
      2. Stage hogging
      3. Selective listening
      4. Insulated listening
      5. Defensive listening
      6. Ambushing
      7. Insensitive listening
   B. **Why We Don't Listen Better**
      1. Message overload

        2. Preoccupation
        3. Rapid thought
        4. Effort
        5. External noise
        6. Faulty assumptions
        7. Lack of apparent advantages
        8. Lack of training
        9. Hearing problems
    C. **Meeting the Challenge of Listening Better**
        1. Talk less
        2. Get rid of distractions
        3. Don't judge prematurely
        4. Look for key ideas

IV. **TYPES OF LISTENING RESPONSES**
    A. **Prompting**
    B. **Questioning**
        1. Ask sincere questions
        2. Avoid counterfeit questions that
            a. trap the speaker
            b. tag questions
            c. make statements
            d. carry hidden agendas
            e. seek "correct" answers
            f. are based on unchecked assumptions
    C. **Paraphrasing**
        1. Factual information
        2. Personal information
            a. change the speaker's wording
            b. offer an example
            c. reflect the underlying theme
        3. When to paraphrase
            a. if the problem is complex enough

© 2014 Cengage Learning. All Rights Reserved. May not be copied, scanned, or duplicated, in whole or in part, except for use as permitted in a license distributed with a certain product or service or otherwise on a password-protected website for classroom use.

   b. if you have necessary time
    and concern

   c. withhold judgment

   d. if it is proportional

D. Supporting

  1. Types

   a. empathizing agreement

   b. offers to help

   c. praise

   d. reassurance

  2. Cold comfort

   a. denying others the right to
    their feelings

   b. minimizing the significance
    of the situation

   c. focusing on "then and
    there" not "here and now"

   d. casting judgment

   e. defending yourself

  3. Guidelines

   a. approval not necessary

   b. monitor reactions

   c. support may not always be
    welcome

   d. be ready for the
    consequences

E. Analyzing

  1. Be tentative

  2. Have a receptive other

  3. Be sure your motives are to help

F. Advising

  1. Is the advice needed?

  2. Is the advice wanted?

  3. Is the advice given in the right
   sequence?

  4. Is the advice coming from an
   expert?

  5. Is the advisor a close and
   trusted person?

6. Is the advice offered in a sensitive, face-saving manner?	
G. Judging	
1. Negative judgments	
2. Constructive criticism	
a. the person should have requested an evaluation	
b. the intent of your judgment should be genuinely constructive	
H. Choosing the Best Listening Response	
1. Gender	
2. The situation	
3. The other person	
4. Your personal style	

KEY TERMS

advising
ambushing
analyzing
attending
counterfeit questions
defensive listening
hearing
insensitive listening
insulated listening
judging
listening
listening fidelity
mindful listening
mindless listening
paraphrasing

prompting
pseudolistening
questioning
remembering
responding
selective listening
sincere questions
stage-hogging
supporting
understanding

ACTIVITIES

7.1 LISTENING DIARY

LEARNING OBJECTIVES

- Identify the situations in which you listen mindfully and those when you listen mindlessly, and evaluate the appropriateness of each style in a given situation.
- Identify the circumstances in which you listen ineffectively, and the poor listening habits you use in these circumstances.

BACKGROUND

Looking Out/Looking In identifies several styles of effective and ineffective listening that you can use when listening to others:

pseudolistening	insensitive listening	supporting
stage hogging	ambushing	analyzing
selective listening	prompting	advising
insulated listening	questioning	judging
defensive listening	paraphrasing	

INSTRUCTIONS

1. Use the following form to record the listening styles you use in various situations.
2. After completing your diary, record your conclusions.

TIME AND PLACE	PEOPLE	SUBJECT	LISTENING STYLE(S)	CONSEQUENCES
EXAMPLE *Saturday night party*	*My date and several new acquaintances*	*Good backpacking trips*	*Stage-hogging: I steered everybody's remarks around to my own experiences*	*I guess I was trying to get everyone to like me, but my egotistical attitude probably accomplished the opposite.*
1.				

TIME AND PLACE	PEOPLE	SUBJECT	LISTENING STYLE(S)	CONSEQUENCES
2.				
3.				
4.				

Based on your observations, what styles of effective and ineffective listening do you use most often? In what situations do you use each of these styles? (Consider the people involved, the time, subject, and your personal mood when determining situational variables.)

_____

_____

_____

What are the consequences of using the listening styles you have just described?

_____

_____

_____

What other listening styles might increase your effectiveness? Why?

_____

_____

_____

7.2 EFFECTIVE QUESTIONING

LEARNING OBJECTIVES

- Identify the response styles that you commonly use when listening to others.
- Demonstrate a combination of listening styles you could use to respond effectively in a given situation.

INSTRUCTIONS

1. For each of the following statements, write two questions to get more information. Avoid counterfeit questions that trap the speaker, carry hidden agendas, seek "correct" answers, or are based on unchecked assumptions.
2. Enter statement examples of your own and two questions each to solicit information.

EXAMPLE

"It's not fair that I have to work so much. Other students can get better grades because they have the time to study."
How do you feel when others score higher than you?
How many hours a week do you work?

1. "I guess it's OK for you to use my computer, but you have to understand that I've put a lot of time and money into it."

   _____

   _____

2. "You'll have the best chance at getting a loan for the new car you want if you give us a complete financial statement and credit history."

   _____

   _____

3. (Instructor to student) "This paper shows a lot of promise. It could probably earn you an A grade if you just develop the idea about the problems that arise from poor listening a bit more."

   _____

   _____

4. "I do like the communication course, but it's not at all what I expected. It's much more *personal,* if you know what I mean."

_____

_____

5. "We just got started on your car's transmission. I'm pretty sure we can have it ready tonight."

_____

_____

6. "I do think it's wrong to take any lives, but sometimes I think certain criminals deserve capital punishment."

_____

_____

7. "My son never tells me what's going on in his life. And now he's moving away."

_____

_____

8. "My family is so controlling. They make it impossible for me to escape."

_____

_____

9. "It was a great game, I guess.   I played a lot, but only scored once. The coach put Ryan in ahead of me."

_____

_____

10. "We had a great evening last night. The dinner was fantastic; so was the party. We saw lots of people. Erin loves that sort of thing."

_____

_____

11. (Your example)_____

    _____

    _____

12. (Your example)_____

    _____

    _____

7.3 PARAPHRASING

LEARNING OBJECTIVES

- • Demonstrate a combination of listening styles you could use to respond effectively in a given situation.

BACKGROUND

The most helpful paraphrasing responses reflect both the speaker's thoughts and feelings. In order for this style of helping to be effective, you also have to sound like yourself, and not another person or a robot. There are many ways to reflect another's thoughts and feelings:

"It sounds like you're . . ."   "And so . . . "
"I hear you saying . . ."   "Is it that . . . "
"Let me see if I've got it. You're saying . . ."   "Are you . . ."
"So you're telling me . . ."   "Could you mean . . . "

Leave your paraphrase open (tentative) by using words that invite the speaker to clarify or correct your paraphrase (ex: "Is that right?")

INSTRUCTIONS

Write a paraphrasing response for each of the statements that follow. Be sure that the response fits your style of speaking, while at the same time it reflects the speaker's *thoughts* and *feelings*.

EXAMPLE

"Stan always wants to tell me about the woman he's currently going out with or the project he's currently working on. He gives me details that take hours, but he rarely asks about who I'm going out with or what I'm interested in."

"It seems like you might be tired (feeling) of hearing about Stan's love life (thoughts) and maybe a little
put-out (feeling) that he doesn't solicit information from you about whom you're dating (thoughts)—
is that it?"

---

1. "I hate this instructor. First she told me my paper was too short, so I gave her more information. Now she tells me it's too wordy."

_____

_____

_____

2. "I worked up that whole study—did all the surveying, the compiling, the writing. It was my idea in the first place. But he turned it in to the head office with his name on it, and he got the credit."

_____

_____

_____

3. "We can't decide whether to put Grandmother in a nursing home. She hates the idea, but she can't take care of herself anymore, and it's just too much for us."

_____

_____

_____

4. "She believed everything he said about me. She wouldn't even listen to my side—just started yelling at me. I thought we were better friends than that."

_____

_____

_____

5. "I'm really starting to hate my job. Every day I do the same boring, mindless work. But if I quit, I might not find any better work."

_____

_____

_____

6. "My girlfriend hasn't called me in forever. I think she must be mad at me."

_____

_____

_____

7. "How can I tell him how I really feel? He might get mad, and then we'd start arguing. He'll think I don't love him if I tell him my real feelings. I'm at a loss."

_____

_____

_____

8. "Why don't you try to be a little less messy around here? This place looks like a dump to all our friends."

_____

_____

_____

9. "There's no reasoning with him. All he cares about is his image—not all the work I have to do to cover for him."

_____

_____

_____

10. "You'd think someone who loves you would take off to be with you now and then, wouldn't you?"

_____

_____

_____

11. "This new software program is supposed to save time? That's a joke."

_____

_____

_____

176

12. "He acts as if staying home with two children all day is easy. I'm more tired now than when I worked full-time – and I got paid then and had weekends and evenings off!"

_____

_____

_____

13. "My father is so needy since my mother died. I have no life of my own."

_____

_____

_____

14. "Group projects are a nightmare. There should be a warning sign for classes that require them."

_____

_____

_____

177

7.4 LISTENING CHOICES

LEARNING OBJECTIVES

- Demonstrate a combination of listening styles you could use to respond effectively in a given situation.
- Identify the response styles that you commonly use when listening to others.

INSTRUCTIONS

For each of the problem statements below, write a response in each style of helping discussed in *Looking Out/Looking In*. Make your response as realistic as possible. Then record a situation of your own and write listening responses for it.

EXAMPLE

"I don't know what to do. I tried to explain to my professor why the assignment was late, but he wouldn't even listen to me."

Prompting (*Short silence*): *And so . . . ? (Look expectantly at partner).*

Questioning: *What did he say? Can you make up the assignment? How do you feel about this?*

Paraphrasing: *You sound really discouraged, since he didn't even seem to care about your reasons—is*
that it?

Supporting: *All of your work has been so good that I'm sure this one assignment won't matter. Don't worry!*

Analyzing: *I think the reason he wasn't sympathetic is because he hears lots of excuses this time of year.*

Advising: *You ought to write him a note. He might be more open if he has time to read it and think*
about it.

Judging: *You have to accept these things. Moping won't do any good, so quit feeling sorry for yourself.*

---

1. My girlfriend says she wants to date other guys this summer while I'm away, working construction. She claims it's just to keep busy and that it won't make any difference with us, but I think she wants to break off permanently, and she's trying to do it gently.

   Prompting _____

Questioning _____

_____

Paraphrasing _____

_____

Supporting _____

_____

Analyzing _____

_____

Advising _____

_____

Judging _____

_____

Which listening styles do you think are most appropriate in this situation? Why?

_____

_____

Which listening styles do you think are most inappropriate in this situation? Why?

_____

_____

2. My roommate and I can't seem to get along. She's always having her boyfriend over, and he doesn't know when to go home. I don't want to move out, but I can't put up with this much longer. If I bring it up I know my roommate will get defensive, though.

Prompting _____

Questioning _____

_____

179

Paraphrasing _____

_____

Supporting _____

_____

Analyzing _____

_____

Advising _____

_____

Judging _____

_____

Which listening styles do you think are most appropriate in this situation? Why?

_____

_____

Which listening styles do you think are most inappropriate in this situation? Why?

_____

_____

3.   The pressure of going to school and doing all the other things in my life is really getting to

me. I can't go on like this, but I don't know where I can cut back. What would be your long and

short term goals in this situation? _____

_____

Circle the type of response you think will help you meet your goals: {Prompting, questioning,

paraphrasing, supporting, analyzing, advising, judging} Why do you think this is the best type of

listening response? _____

Now write this type of response. _____

_____

4.   You think that by the time you become an adult your parents would stop treating you like a

child, but not mine! If I wanted their advice about how to live my life, I'd ask.

What would be your long and short term goals in this situation?

_____

_____

Circle the type of response you think will help you meet your goals: {Prompting, questioning,

paraphrasing, supporting, analyzing, advising, judging} Why do you think this is the best type

of listening response? _____

        _____

Now write this type of response. _____

_____

5. (record a situation of your own here) _____

        _____

What would be your long and short term goals in this situation?

_____

_____

Circle the type of response you think will help you meet your goals: {Prompting, questioning,

paraphrasing, supporting, analyzing, advising, judging} Why do you think this is the best type of

listening response? _____

Now write this type of response. _____

_____

Reflections

1. Are there types of listening responses that you are familiar with that are not mentioned here?

    _____

    _____

    _____

2. Are there listening responses that you have trouble categorizing? Which ones? Why are they difficult to categorize?

    _____

    _____

    _____

3. Is there value to learning these categories? Why or why not?

    _____

    _____

    _____

7.5 LISTENING ANALYSIS

LEARNING OBJECTIVES

- Identify the response styles that you commonly use when listening to others.
- Demonstrate a combination of listening styles you could use to respond effectively in a given situation.

INSTRUCTIONS

Use the case below and the discussion questions that follow to discuss the variety of communication issues involved in effective communication. Make notes on this page, add other pages on your own, or prepare a group report/analysis based on your discussion. Add your own experiences to individualize the analysis.

CASE

Larry and Sam have been friends since elementary school and are now in their thirties. Larry has been happily married for ten years. Sam has been engaged four times, and each time has broken it off as the marriage date approaches. Sam has just announced another engagement.

1. What are the likely barriers that would prevent Larry from listening effectively?

   _____

   _____

2. What types of ineffective listening are likely to occur if Larry doesn't carefully consider his listening options?

   _____

   _____

3. What listening style(s) could Larry use that would be most helpful to Sam? Why? Construct a response for Larry using that style.

   _____

   _____

4. Suppose that the two friends described here are both women. How would your responses to the preceding questions change?

7.6 ASSESSING LISTENING SITUATIONS

LEARNING OBJECTIVES

- Demonstrate a combination of listening styles you could use to respond effectively in a given situation.

Instructions

We all face challenges in listening to others. Read the following scenarios below and describe what strategy you would use to maintain effective listening.

1. You are trying to talk to your friend about problems with her parents while you are at a bar with loud music in the background.

Strategy:

_____

_____

_____

2. Your friend needs to talk to you about her new relationship but you have a difficult time listening because you have an early morning history test to study for and have a trip to plan. With all this on your mind, how can you maintain effective listening?

Strategy:

_____

_____

_____

3. You are talking on your cell phone and the reception is bad.

Strategy:

_____

_____

_____

STUDY GUIDE

CHECK YOUR UNDERSTANDING

True/False

Mark the statements below as true or false. On the lines below each statement, correct the false statements by making a true statement.

_____ 1. We spend more time listening to others than in any other type of communication.

_____

_____ 2. Speaking is active; listening is passive.

_____

_____ 3. All interruptions are attempts at stage-hogging.

_____

_____ 4. Both men and women want supportive, endorsing messages in difficult situations.

_____

_____ 5. Listening skills are just as vital as speaking skills for career success.

_____

_____ 6. People speak at about the same rate as others are capable of understanding their speech.

_____

_____ 7. The advantages of listening are more obvious to people than the advantages of speaking.

_____

_____ 8. Responding to a message rarely involves giving observable feedback to the speaker.

_____

_____ 9. Judging as a listening response may be favorable or negative.

_____

_____ 10. A good listener pays attention to paralanguage.

_____

COMPLETION

Fill in the blanks below with the correct terms chosen from the list below.

residual message   attending   conversational narcissist
sincere question   counterfeit question   constructive criticism
agreement   understanding   remembering
hearing   selective   insulated

1. _____ is a name given to a nonlistening stage-hog.

2. _____ is a genuine request for new information aimed at understanding others.

3. _____ is the information we store (remember) after processing information from teachers, friends, radio, TV, and other sources.

4. _____ is the psychological process of listening.

5. _____ is a query that is a disguised attempt to send a message, not receive one.

6. _____ is a lesser form of negative judgment which is intended to help the problem-holder improve in the future.

7. _____ is the physiological process of listening.

8. _____ is the process of making sense of a message.

9. _____ is the ability to recall information.

10. _____ is a listening response designed to show solidarity with speakers by telling them how right they are.

11. _____ is a nonlistening style that responds only to what the listener cares about.

187

12. _____ is a nonlistening style that ignores information the listener doesn't to deal with.

MULTIPLE CHOICE

Match the letter of the listening type with its example found below.

a. advising   c. analyzing   e. supporting   g. paraphrasing
b. judging   d. questioning   f. prompting

_____ 1. "So what do you mean by that?"

_____ 2. "You're mad at me for postponing the meeting?"

_____ 3. "You're probably just more upset than usual because of the stress of exams."

_____ 4. "What reason did she give for not attending?"

_____ 5. "Well, that was good of him not to complain."

_____ 6. "Have you tried praising her?"

_____ 7. "Have you tried talking to him about it?"

_____ 8. "Are you as excited as you sound about this big meet?"

_____ 9. "Jim should not have said that to Amy after you asked him not to."

_____ 10. "And then what happened?"

_____ 11. "So why did you go to Ellie's in the first place?"

_____ 12. "You really are good; they'll recognize that."

_____ 13. "It's not fair for you to have to work nights."

_____ 14. "Maybe you should give her a taste of her own medicine."

_____ 15. "And so you feel like retaliating because you're hurt?"

_____ 16. "Maybe you're a little insecure because of the divorce?"

_____ 17. "Like what?"

_____ 18. "What makes you think that he's cheating?"

_____ 19. "You've always pulled out those grades before—I know you can do it again."

_____ 20. "She's probably jealous so that's why she's doing that."

Choose the best listening response to each statement below.

21. Boss to employee: "Draft a letter that denies this request for a refund, but make it tactful." Identify the best paraphrasing of content response.

    a. "What do you want me to say?"
    b. "How can I say no tactfully?"

c. "So I should explain nicely why we can't give a refund, right?"

d. "In other words, you want me to give this customer the brush-off?"

22. Friend says, "How do they expect us to satisfy the course requirements when there aren't enough spaces in the classes we're supposed to take?" Identify the best questioning response.

a. "What class do you need that you can't get into?"

b. "You think that some of the courses are worthless—is that it?"

c. "Sounds like you're sorry you chose this major."

d. "Why don't you write a letter to the chairperson of the department?"

23. Friend says, "Why don't I meet you after class at the student union?" Identify the best questioning response.

a. "So you want me to pick you up at the student union?"

b. "You want me to pick you up *again*?"

c. "What time do you think you'll be there?"

d. "Why can't you drive yourself? Is your car broken again?"

24. Co-worker advises, "When you go in for a job interview, be sure and talk about the internship, your coursework, and your extracurricular activities. Don't expect them to ask you." Identify the best paraphrasing response.

a. "You think they won't ask about those things?"

b. "Won't that sound like bragging?"

c. "Why should I talk about the internship?"

d. "So you're saying not to be bashful about stressing my experience?"

25. Friend says, "I don't think it's right that they go out and recruit women when there are plenty of good men around." Identify the best supporting response.

a. "I think you're job-hunting well in spite of the challenges."

b. "You shouldn't let that bother you."

c. "That's just the way life is."

d. "I can see that you're angry. What makes you think women are being given an unfair advantage?"

For each of the statements below, identify which response is the most complete and accurate paraphrasing of the speaker's thoughts and feelings.

26. "Sometimes I think I'd like to drop out of school, but then I start to feel like a quitter."

a. "Maybe it would be helpful to take a break. You can always come back, you know."

b. "You're afraid that you might fail if you stay in school now, is that it?"

c. "I can really relate to what you're saying. I feel awkward here myself sometimes."

d. "So you'd feel ashamed of yourself if you quit now, even though you'd like to?"

27. "I don't want to go to the party. I won't know anyone there, and I'll wind up sitting by myself all night."

    a. "You're anxious about introducing yourself to people who don't know you."
    b. "You never know; you could have a great time."
    c. "So you really don't want to go, eh?"
    d. "What makes you think it will be that way?"

28. "I get really nervous talking to my professor. I keep thinking that I sound stupid."

    a. "Talking to her is really a frightening experience."
    b. "You're saying that you'd rather not approach her."
    c. "You get the idea that she's evaluating you, so you feel inadequate.
    d. "You think that talking to her might affect your grade for the worse."

29. "I don't know what to do about my kids. Their whining is driving me crazy."

    a. "Even though whining is natural, it's getting to you."
    b. "Sometimes you lose patience and feel irritated when they complain."
    c. "You're getting angry at them."
    d. "Even the best parents get irritated sometimes."

30. "I just blew another test in that class. Why can't I do better?"

    a. "You probably need to study harder. You'll get it!"
    b. "You're feeling sorry for yourself because you can't pull a better grade."
    c. "Where do you think the problem is?"
    d. "You're discouraged and frustrated because you don't know what you're doing wrong."

Choose the best answer for each of the statements below:

_____ 31.   A good listener pays attention to
               a. paralanguage.
               b. facial expression.
               c. nonverbal cues.
               d. all of the above.

_____ 32.   When we move beyond hearing and start to listen and process information in two different ways, we are engaging in
               a. dual process theory.
               b. process theory.
               c. critical listening.
               d. careful listening.

_____ 33. In a survey that questioned adults who had spouses with hearing loss,

a. many respondents were unfazed when their partner couldn't hear them correctly.
b. many respondents felt that their spouses are open and upfront about their hearing obstacles.
c. many respondents believed their spouses were in denial about their condition.
d. less than a quarter of respondents felt annoyed when their partner couldn't hear them correctly.

_____ 34. When paraphrasing, it is a good idea to

a. assume your paraphrase is correct.
b. end with a question to confirm the paraphrase was accurate.
c. paraphrase in a variety of ways to ensure accuracy.
d. avoid paraphrasing if it feels awkward.

191

CHAPTER 7 STUDY GUIDE ANSWERS

TRUE/FALSE

1.	T	3.	F	5.	T	7.	F	9.	T
2.	F	4.	T	6.	F	8.	F	10.	T

COMPLETION

1. conversational narcissist
2. sincere question
3. residual message
4. attending
5. counterfeit question
6. constructive criticism
7. hearing
8. understanding
9. remembering
10. agreement
11. selective
12. insulated

MULTIPLE CHOICE

1.	f	7.	a	13.	b	19.	e	25.	a	31.	d
2.	g	8.	g	14.	a	20.	c	26.	d	32.	a
3.	c	9.	b	15.	g	21.	c	27.	a	33.	c
4.	d	10.	f	16.	c	22.	a	28.	c	34.	b
5.	b	11.	d	17.	f	23.	c	29.	b		
6.	a	12.	e	18.	d	24.	d	30.	d		

CHAPTER EIGHT

Communication and Relational Dynamics

OUTLINE

Use this outline to take notes as you read the chapter in the text or as your instructor lectures in class.

I. **WHY WE FORM RELATIONSHIPS**
   A. **Appearance**
   B. **Similarity**
   C. **Complementarity**
   D. **Reciprocal Attraction**
   E. **Competence**
   F. **Disclosure**
   G. **Proximity**
   H. **Rewards**

II. **MODELS OF RELATIONAL DYNAMICS**
   A. **Developmental Perspective**
      1. Initiating
      2. Experimenting
      3. Intensifying
      4. Integrating
      5. Bonding
      6. Differentiating
      7. Circumscribing
      8. Stagnating

193

      9.   Avoiding

      10. Terminating

  B.   **A Dialectical Perspective**

      1.   Connection vs. autonomy

      2.   Openness vs. privacy

      3.   Predictability vs. novelty

      4.   Managing dialectical tensions

       a. denial

       b. disorientation

       c. alternation

       d. segmentation

       e. balance

       f. integration

       g. recalibration

       h. reaffirmation

III. CHARACTERISTICS OF
      RELATIONSHIPS

  A. **Relationships Are Constantly**
      Changing

     1.   Security

     2.   Disintigration

     3.   Alienation

     4.   Resynthesis

     5.   New level of security

  B. **Relationships Are Affected by**
      Culture

III. COMMUNICATING ABOUT
RELATIONSHIPS

  A. **Content and Relational Messages**

     1. Content: subject

     2. Relational: feelings

  B. **Types of Relational Messages**

     1. Affinity

     2. Immediacy

     3. Respect

     4. Control

a. Decisional	
b. Conversational	
C. Metacommunication	

KEY TERMS

affinity
avoiding
bonding
circumscribing
connection-autonomy dialectic
control
dialectical tension
differentiating
experimenting
immediacy

initiating
integrating
intensifying
metacommunication
openness-privacy dialectic
predictability-novelty dialectic
respect
stagnating
terminating

ACTIVITIES

8.1 DISCOVERING DIALECTICS

LEARNING OBJECTIVES

- Describe the dialectical tensions in a given relationship, how they influence communication, and the most effective strategies for managing them.

INSTRUCTIONS

1. Identify the dialectical tensions operating in the situations below, taking time to explain the conflicting feelings and thoughts in each: *connection vs. autonomy, openness vs. privacy, predictability vs. novelty.*
2. Identify one or more of the eight strategies for managing dialectical tensions (*denial, disorientation, alternation, segmentation, balance, integration, recalibration, and reaffirmation)* that you believe would be most beneficial to the relationship, and explain how the relationship would deal with the dialectical tension under these circumstances.
3. Describe dialectical tensions at work in your own relationships and label and explain the strategies that you use to deal with them.

SITUATION	DIALECTICAL TENSION	STRATEGY FOR MANAGING
EXAMPLE: *Sandra, nineteen, and her mother, Tracy, have become good friends over the past few years. Sandra now has a serious boyfriend and spends less time talking to her mother.*	*The open-privacy dialectic is probably at work here. Sandra and Tracy continue to share the intimacy of their mother-daughter relationship, but privacy needs about the boyfriend probably keep them at more distance.*	*Sandra and Tracy are likely to use the segmentation strategy, in which they maintain openness about many areas but keep certain areas of the boyfriend relationship "off limits."*
1. Daryl is new to the software firm where Steve has been for five years. Daryl has asked Steve to play golf this weekend. Steve is uncomfortable about mixing business and pleasure, but still wants to have a good working relationship with Daryl.		

SITUATION	DIALECTICAL TENSION	STRATEGY FOR MANAGING
2. Nesto and Gina have been dating for six months. They continue to enjoy one another's company, but each has begun to notice annoying little habits that the other one has.		
3. Jenner and A. J. are siblings who have always relied on one another completely. Jenner appreciates A. J.'s dependability, but wishes their times together weren't so boring.		
4. Eugenia and Shane have worked at the same business for twenty years. They have collaborated on a number of projects. They've tried to get together socially, but their spouses don't seem to get along.		
5. Christina and Nicole are roommates. Christina wants them to share everything, but Nicole is not proud of a few things she's done and doesn't want to face her friend's judgment.		
6. Your example:		
7. Your example:		

197

8.2 RELATIONAL STAGES

LEARNING OBJECTIVES

- Identify factors that have influenced your choice of relational partners.
- Use Knapp's model to describe the nature of communication in the various stages of a relationship.
- Describe the dialectical tensions in a given relationship, how they influence communication, and the most effective strategies for managing them.

INSTRUCTIONS

1. Discuss the various situations listed below.
2. Identify the relational stage(s) that many of these behaviors illustrate (e.g., initiating, experimenting, intensifying, integrating, bonding, differentiating, circumscribing, avoiding, stagnating, terminating).
3. Cite a brief passage from chapter 8 that verifies the stage of the relationship.
4. Record relational situations of your own in the same manner.

EXAMPLE

Two friends are discussing the effects of divorce in their families.
Relational stage illustrated: *This type of self-disclosure would most likely occur in an intensifying stage of a relationship, where the friends have gone beyond the small talk of experimenting and are beginning to develop more trust, more depth rather than breadth of self-disclosure, and where secrets are told and favors given.*

1. Two friends are telling one another about using/refusing drugs.

   Relational stage illustrated _____
   Cite a brief passage to verify the stage of the relationship

   _____

   _____

   _____

2. Two classmates are comparing the results of their first exam.

   Relational stage illustrated _____

   Cite a brief passage to verify the stage of the relationship

   _____

   _____

3. Two people seated next to each other on an overseas flight begin telling one another about their past romantic involvements.

Relational stage illustrated _____

Cite a brief passage to verify the stage of the relationship

_____

_____

_____

4. Two long-term friends are discussing their worries and feelings of responsibility regarding their parents' advancing age.

Relational stage illustrated _____

Cite a brief passage to verify the stage of the relationship

_____

_____

5. Cousins who practically lived at each other's homes as teenagers five years ago, now seem to have nothing to talk about.

Relational stage illustrated _____

Cite a brief passage to verify the stage of the relationship

_____

_____

6. A divorced couple meets briefly to discuss education and vacation plans for their children.
Relational stage illustrated _____

Cite a brief passage to verify the stage of the relationship

_____

_____

7. A man and woman who dated for six months during college ten years ago now find themselves working for the same company.

Relational stage illustrated _____

Cite a brief passage to verify the stage of the relationship

_____

_____

8. A manager and employee have agreed to sit down and talk about the problems they are experiencing with each other.

Relational stage illustrated _____

Cite a brief passage to verify the stage of the relationship

_____

_____

9. Your example: _____

Relational stage illustrated _____

Cite a brief passage to verify the stage of the relationship

_____

_____

10. Your example: _____

Relational stage illustrated _____

Cite a brief passage to verify the stage of the relationship

_____

_____

8.3 RECOGNIZING RELATIONAL MESSAGES

LEARNING OBJECTIVES

- Identify the content and relational dimensions of communication in a given transaction.

INSTRUCTIONS

1. Read each message below. Picture in your mind the nonverbal behaviors that accompany each of the statements.
2. Describe the relational issues that seem to be involved in each of the situations. Use your text to *label and explain* the relational dimensions of **affinity, immediacy, respect and control** shown by the speaker in each example.

MESSAGE CONTENT	RELATIONAL DIMENSION (affinity, immediacy, respect, control)
Example: You tell your romantic partner, " . . . Anyhow, that's what I think. What do you think?"	*High in immediacy because I invite involvement and show interest by my tone.* *High in affinity as I show liking by my eye contact and touch.*
Example: Your instructor invites the class to, "Tell me what's working and what isn't."	*Low in control as the instructor invites influence over how the course is run.* *High in respect by valuing the opinions of students.*
1. You ask a friend to come over and the reply is, "I'm sorry, but I have to work."	
2. Someone you live with complains, "You don't help out enough around the house."	
3. Your roommate says, "You're no fun. I think I'm going to bed."	
4. Your boss asks, "Are your hours working out?"	

201

MESSAGE CONTENT	RELATIONAL DIMENSION (affinity, immediacy, respect, control)
5. Your boss says, "You'll need a doctor's note to verify your illness."	
6. Your friend teases, "You can't seem to remember the important stuff."	
7. Your parent says, "I know you'll make the right decision."	
8. Your romantic partner says, "I need you to let me know where you are."	
9. Someone reminds you, "Drive carefully."	
10. A family member says you should spend more time at home and you reply, "I'll do what I please."	
11. The doctor's receptionist says, "Can you hold, please?" when you call to make an appointment.	
12. You are getting ready to leave and your partner says, "You're going to wear *that*?"	
13. A friend says, "Fine" and hangs up the phone.	
14. When you ask if you can take time off, your boss rolls her eyes and sighs, "Again?"	
15. You tell your friend you don't feel well, and the response is, "Had too good a time last night?"	

8.4 Forming Relationships

LEARNING OBJECTIVES

* Identify factors that have influenced your choice of relational partners.

INSTRUCTIONS

Identify three relationships. First, list the type of relationship (friend, significant relationship, family member, etc). Then identify three relationship-forming factors (appearance, similarity, complementarity, disclosure, etc). Finally, describe how these three factors helped you form that relationship.

Relationship type 1: _____

Relationship forming factors: _____

Description:

_____

_____

_____

_____

Relationship type 2: _____

Relationship forming factors: _____

Description :

_____

_____

_____

Relationship type 3: _____

Relationship forming factors: _____

Description:

_____

_____

_____

8.5 Applying Knapp's Model

LEARNING OBJECTIVES:

- Use Knapp's model to describe the nature of communication in the various stages of a relationship.

INSTRUCTIONS: Think of a romantic or close relationship that you had that ended in termination. Describe in the spaces below how your relationship fulfilled Knapp's model of communication.

Initiating:

_____

_____

_____

Experimenting:

_____

_____

_____

Intensifying:

_____

_____

_____

Integrating:

_____

_____

Bonding:

_____

_____

Differentiating:

_____

_____

_____

Circumscribing:

_____

_____

_____

Stagnating:

_____

_____

_____

Avoiding:

_____

_____

_____

Terminating:

_____

_____

_____

STUDY GUIDE
CHECK YOUR UNDERSTANDING

TRUE/FALSE

Mark the statements below as true or false. Correct statements that are false on the lines below to create a true statement.

_____ 1. Romantic partners create positive illusions of one another and view each other as more attractive over time.

_____ 2. The stage-related model advocates maintenance in relationships, whereas the dialectical model emphasizes commitment.

_____ 3. Forgiveness usually increases emotional distress and aggression.

_____ 4. Lack of eye contact and increased distance from someone are ways to communicate immediacy.

_____ 5. E-mail is not helpful in maintaining interpersonal relationships.

_____ 6. The struggle to achieve important, but seemingly incompatible goals in relationships, results in the creation of dialectical tension.

_____ 7. The struggle between independence and dependence in a relationship is called the openness-privacy dialectic.

_____ 8. "I like the way we don't discuss our political differences in public" is an example of metacommunication.

_____ 9. The best chance for righting a wrong is taking responsibility for your transgression.

_____ 10. Relational partners often go through evolving cycles in which they can repeat a relational stage at a new level.

_____

_____ 11. Research suggests that even when forgiven, transgressors are as likely to repeat their offenses as those who have not received forgiveness.

_____

_____ 12. Relational commitment involves a promise to remain in a relationship, sometimes explicitly, sometimes implied.

_____

COMPLETION

Fill in the blanks below with the correct terms chosen from the list below.

dialectical   positivity   relational transgression
openness   attraction variable   metacommunication
forgiveness   immediacy   appearance
complementarity

1. _____ The messages people exchange about their communication; communication about communication.

2. _____ A relational maintenance strategy of keeping the relational climate upbeat and avoiding disapproval or unconstructive remarks.

3. _____ A strategy to maintain a relationship that involves talking directly about the relationship and disclosing needs and concerns.

4. _____ is an explanation for what makes us want to develop personal relationships with some people and not with others.

5. _____ A violation of the explicit or implicit terms of the relationship.

6. _____ A method of relational repair that promotes physical and emotional health.

7. _____ An attraction variable that is most important at the beginning of relationships, and less important over time.

8. _____ An attraction variable in which people are different in ways that meet each of their needs.

9. _____ A relational message that conveys involvement and interest.

10. _____ is a tension that arises when two incompatible goals exist in a relationship.

MULTIPLE CHOICE

Place the letter of the developmental stage of the relationship on the line before its example found below.

a. initiating
b. experimenting
c. intensifying
d. integrating
e. bonding

f. differentiating
g. circumscribing
h. stagnating
i. avoiding
j. terminating

_____ 1. A public ritual marks this stage.

_____ 2. First glances and "sizing up" each other typifies this stage.

_____ 3. Called the "we" stage, this stage involves increasing self-disclosure.

_____ 4. Lots of "small talk" typifies this stage.

_____ 5. This stage involves much focus on individual rather than dyadic interests.

_____ 6. There's very little growth or experimentation in this stage.

_____ 7. This stage involves much behavior that talks around the relational issues because the partners expect bad feelings.

_____ 8. The partners' social circles merge at this stage and they make purchases or commitments together.

_____ 9. No attempts are made to contact the other at this stage.

_____ 10. The relationship is redefined or dissolved at this stage.

_____ 11. A marriage ceremony would be typical here.

_____ 12. Roommates who make sure they are never in the same room and who are tolerating one another only until the lease is up might be at this stage.

_____ 13. A couple who avoids talking about future commitment because they are afraid of how the discussion will go is probably at this stage.

Choose the best answer for each of the statements below:

_____ 14. Research suggests attraction to partners who have complementary temperament is rooted in

a. family history.

b. socialization.
c. biology.
d. communication styles.

_____ 15. Revealing personal information only when you are sure the other person is trustworthy is a practice in

a. self protection.
b. self privacy.
c. self defense.
d. self disclosure.

_____ 16. In the early stages of a relationship, _____ is especially important.

a. meta communication
b. a positive illusion
c. behavior
d. appearance

CHAPTER 8 STUDY GUIDE ANSWERS

TRUE/FALSE

1. T	4. F	7. F	10. T
2. F	5. F	8. T	11. F
3. F	6. T	9. T	12. T

COMPLETION

1. metacommunication
2. positivity
3. openness
4. attraction variable
5. relational transgression
6. forgiveness
7. appearance
8. complementarity
9. immediacy
10. dialectical

MULTIPLE CHOICE

1. e	4. b	7. g	10. j	13. g	16. d
2. a	5. f	8. d	11. e	14. c	
3. c	6. h	9. i	12. i	15. a	

CHAPTER NINE

Interpersonal Communication in Close Relationships

OUTLINE

Use this outline to take notes as you read the chapter in the text or as your instructor lectures in class.

I. INTIMACY IN CLOSE RELATIONSHIPS	_____
A. The Dimensions of Intimacy	
1. Physical	_____
2. Intellectual	
3. Emotional	_____
4. Shared activities	
B. Masculine and Feminine Intimacy Styles	_____
1. Women tend to value talk to develop intimacy	_____
2. Men tend to value activities to develop intimacy	_____
3. Gender role not biological sex influences intimacy styles	_____
C. Cultural Influences on Intimacy	_____
1. Historical	
2. Regional cultures	_____
a. individualist	
b. collectivist	_____
3. Co-cultures and class	

D. **Intimacy in Mediated Communication**

    1. Speed of intimacy development through mediated communication

    2. Importance of mediated communication in contemporary relationships

E. **Limits of Intimacy**

    1. Diminishing returns

    2. Necessity of nonintimate relationships

II. **COMMUNICATION IN FAMILIES**

  A. **Characteristics of Family Communication**

    1. Family communication is formative

      a. attachment theory

      b. birth order

    2. Family communication is role-driven

    3. Family communication is involuntary

  B. **Families as Systems**

    1. Family systems are interdependent

    2. Family systems are manifested through communication

    3. Family systems are nested

    4. Families are more than the sum of their parts

  C. **Communication Patterns Within Families**

    1. Conversation orientation

      a. high conversation orientation

      b. low conversation orientation

    2. Conformity orientation

            3. Family communication pattern
               a. consensual
               b. pluralistic
               c. protective
               d. laissez-faire

III. COMMUNICATION IN FRIENDSHIPS
   ### A. Types of Friendships
      1. Youthful versus mature
      2. Long term versus short term
      3. Relationship oriented versus task oriented
      4. High disclosure versus low disclosure
      5. High obligation versus low obligation
      6. Frequent contact versus occasional contact
   ### B. Sex, Gender, and Friendship
      1. Same-sex friendships
      2. Cross-sex friendships
      3. Friends with benefits
      4. Gender considerations
   ### C. Friendship and Social Media

IV. COMMUNICATION IN ROMANTIC RELATIONSHIPS
   ### A. Romantic Turning Points
   ### B. Couples Conflict Styles
      1. Volatile
      2. Avoidant
      3. Validating
   ### C. Languages of Love
      1. Words of affirmation
      2. Quality time
      3. Gifts
      4. Acts of service
      5. Physical touch

213

V. IMPROVING CLOSE RELATIONSHIPS
    A. Relational Commitment
    B. Relationships Require Maintenance and Support
        1. Relational maintenance
           a. positivity
           b. openness
           c. assurances
           d. social networks
           e. sharing tasks
        2. Social support
           a. emotional support
           b. informational support
           c. instrumental support
    C. Repairing Damaged Relationships
        1. Types of relational transgressions
           a. minor vs. significant
           b. social vs. relational
           c. deliberate vs. unintentional
           d. one-time vs. incremental
        2. Strategies for relational repair
           a. acknowledgement
           b. apology
           c. compensation
        3. Forgiving transgressions

KEY TERMS

conformity orientation
conversation orientation
relational maintenance
family communication
relational transgression
social support
love languages

relational commitment
family system
relational turning point
friends with benefits
intimacy

ACTIVITIES

9.1 ASSESSING SELF-CONCEPT AND FAMILY COMMUNICATION

LEARNING OBJECTIVES

- Describe the relationship between self-concept, self-esteem, and communication.
- Compare and contrast the perceived self and the presenting self as they relate to identity management.

INSTRUCTIONS

Family plays an important role in developing our self-concepts and self-esteem. Answer the following questions about your family below. Indicate how the information about your family has contributed to your self-concept.

1. What are some of your family values?

_____

_____

_____

2. How does your family communicate with each other?

_____

_____

_____

3. What physical traits does your family have?

_____

_____

4. How has your family contributed to your self-esteem?

_____

215

_____

_____

Now that you have assessed how your family has influenced your self-concept, interview a friend and ask them the same questions about their family. Record their answers and compare and contrast the similarities and differences between your families on the next page.

1. What are some of your family values?

_____

_____

_____

2. How does your family communicate with each other?

_____

_____

_____

3. What physical traits does your family have?

_____

_____

4. How has your family influenced your self-esteem?

_____

_____

Now list the similarities and differences between you and your friend.

SIMILARITIES   **DIFFERENCES**

216

9.2 RELATIONAL DYNAMICS

LEARNING OBJECTIVES

- Outline the potential benefits and risks of disclosing in a selected situation.

INSTRUCTIONS

Use the case below and the discussion questions that follow to discuss the variety of communication issues involved in effective communication. Make notes on this page, add other pages on your own, or prepare a group report/analysis based on your discussion. Add your own experiences to individualize the analysis.

CASE

Alora and Malcolm dated one another exclusively for three years. They broke up for six months, and now are back together and talking about getting married. While they were broken up, Alora became intimate with a casual friend of Malcolm's for a brief time before she realized that she really loved only Malcolm. During this same time period, Malcolm dated around; but he did not get serious about any one. Malcolm has now told Alora that he believes they should tell one another everything about the time they were apart.

1. Do you think full self-disclosure is important in this relationship? Why or why not?

   _____

   _____

2. Use other relationships (your own and others) to evaluate how important full self-disclosure is to committed relationships. Cite times when full disclosure may be more harmful than helpful?

   _____

   _____

3. Evaluate the alternatives to self-disclosure in this situation. Explain how lies, benevolent lies, partial disclosure, equivocation, or hinting might be more effective than full disclosure?

   _____

   _____

4. Using quotations from the text, evaluate how much Alora and Malcolm should disclose to each other about the six months they were apart.

9.3 ASSESSING CULTURAL AND GENDER INFLUENCES ON INTIMACY IN INTERPERSONAL RELATIONSHIPS

LEARNING OBJECTIVES

- Identify the dimensions of intimacy that operate and how they are expressed in a specific relationship.
- Explain the need for both intimacy and distance in a given relationship.

INSTRUCTIONS

Interview a classmate who is a different gender or is from another culture; ask the following questions about how the dimensions of intimacy influence their relationship. Record their answers to the following questions below. Ask yourself the same questions, and record your own answers.

QUESTIONS FOR CLASSMATE

Relationship description: (boyfriend/girlfriend, parent/child, etc.)_____

What role does physical intimacy play in your relationship?

_____

_____

What role does intellectual intimacy play in your relationship?

_____

_____

What role does emotional intimacy play in your relationship?

_____

_____

What role do shared activities play in your relationship?

_____

_____

Why is intimacy needed in your relationship?

_____

_____

Why is there a need for distance in your relationship?

_____

_____

QUESTIONS FOR YOU

Relationship description: (boyfriend/girlfriend, parent/child, etc.)_____

What role does physical intimacy play in your relationship?

_____

_____

What role does intellectual intimacy play in your relationship?

_____

_____

What role does emotional intimacy play in your relationship?

_____

_____

What role do shared activities play in your relationship?

_____

_____

Why is intimacy needed in your relationship?

_____

_____

Why is there a need for distance in your relationship?

_____

_____

Now that you have interviewed your classmate on the dimensions of intimacy in their relationship, compare your answers to theirs on the worksheet below and on the next page. Indicate how culture or gender may have contributed to any differences.

SIMILARITIES	DIFFERENCES	HOW CULTURE OR GENDER MIGHT CONTRIBUTE
Physical:	Physical:	
Intellectual:	Intellectual:	
Emotional:	Emotional:	

220

SIMILARITIES	DIFFERENCES	HOW CULTURE OR GENDER MIGHT CONTRIBUTE
Shared activities:	Shared activities:	
Need for intimacy:	Need for intimacy:	
Need for distance:	Need for distance:	

STUDY GUIDE

CHECK YOUR UNDERSTANDING

TRUE/FALSE

Mark the statements below as true or false. Correct statements that are false on the lines below to create a true statement.

_____ 1. Intimacy is definitely rewarding, so maximizing intimacy is the best way of relating to others.

_____

_____ 2. Catharsis can provide mental and emotional relief.

_____

_____ 3. Research shows that male-male relationships involve less disclosure than male-female or female-female relationships.

_____

_____ 4. Using IM or Facebook, or writing in a blog, is a way to enhance intimacy in interpersonal relationships.

_____

_____ 5. Relational intimacy may develop more quickly through mediated channels than face to face communication.

_____

_____ 6. Less than truthful communication is uncommon in the closest of relationships.

_____

_____ 7. In a casual relationship, the depth of self-disclosure may be great, but not the breadth.

_____

_____ 8. Self-disclosure usually leads to reciprocity.

_____

_____ 9. Physical intimacy is sexual and is always connected with a close interpersonal relationship.

_____

222

_____ 10. People justify over half of their lies as ways to avoid embarrassment for themselves or others.

_____

_____ 11. Sexual intimacy is always associated with a close relationship.

_____

COMPLETION

Fill in the blanks below with the correct terms chosen from the list below.

suprasystem	role	attachment theory	intellectual
physical	emotional	hinting	personal preference

1. _____ is the type of intimacy that comes from an exchange of important ideas.

2. _____ is the type of intimacy that comes from touching, struggling, or sex.

3. _____ is the type of intimacy that comes from exchanging important feelings.

4. _____ is an explanation for what makes us want to develop personal relationships with some people and not with others.

5. _____ argues that children develop bonds either secure or insecure with family members.

6. A _____ is a set of expectations about how to communicate.

7. Families are also members or larger _____.

8. _____ is an alternative to self-disclosure in which the person gives only a clue to the direct meaning of the response.

MULTIPLE CHOICE

1. Which of these is *not* a dimension of intimacy in interpersonal relationships?
    a. physical
    b. shared activities
    c. chronological
    d. emotional

2. Researchers have found that in a "friends with benefits" situation people
    a. always form romantic relationships.
    b. never form romantic relationships.
    c. are afraid to develop feelings for the other person because they might be unreciprocated.
    d. have no feelings for the other person.

3. Self-disclosure, by definition, is all of these except
    a. intentional.
    b. significant.
    c. not known by others.
    d. accidental.

4. Self-disclosure can be all of these except
    a. impossible.
    b. insignificant.
    c. significant.
    d. accidental.

5. "Friends with benefits" deals specifically with friends who also
    a. engage in physical intimacy.
    b. dislike one another without saying.
    c. are part of a family dynamic.
    d. engage in significant emotional and intellectual intimacy.

6. Which of these is a dimension of intimacy in interpersonal relationships?
    a. ignoring the other person
    b. shared activities
    c. shutting down when your partner begins to self-disclose
    d. using the word "feel" as much as possible

7. Fear of intimacy can cause major problems in
    a. creating relationships .
    b. sustaining relationships.
    c. a and b
    d. none of the above

8. Self-validation, identity management, and relationship maintenance have been identified as reasons why people
    a. self-disclose.
    b. reject intimacy.
    c. create relationships.
    d. create relational tensions.

9. According to the text, people want
   a. ten to twelve close relationships in their lives.
   b. one to two close relationships in their lives.
   c. four to six close relationships in their lives.
   d. two to three close relationships in their lives.

10. Self-disclosure
   a. usually occurs in large groups.
   b. usually occurs incrementally.
   c. is generally coerced, not voluntary.
   d. is the only ethical response in most situations.

CHAPTER 9 STUDY GUIDE ANSWERS

TRUE/FALSE

1.	F	4.	T	7.	F	10.	T
2.	T	5.	T	8.	T	11.	F
3.	T	6.	F	9.	F		

COMPLETION

1. intellectual
2. physical
3. emotional
4. personal preference

5. attachment theory
6. role
7. suprasystem
8. hinting

MULTIPLE CHOICE

1.	c	4.	a	7.	c	10.	b
2.	c	5.	a	8.	a		
3.	d	6.	b	9.	c		

CHAPTER TEN

Improving Communication Climates

OUTLINE

Use this outline to take notes as you read the chapter in the text and/or as your instructor lectures in class.

I. **COMMUNICATION CLIMATE AND CONFIRMING MESSAGES**	
A. Levels of Message Confirmation	
1. Confirming communication	
a. recognition	
b. acknowledgement	
c. endorsement	
2. Disconfirming communication	
a. impervious responses	
b. interrupting	
c. irrelevant responses	
d. tangential responses	
e. impersonal responses	
f. ambiguous responses	
g. incongruous responses	
3. Disagreeing messages	
a. aggressiveness	
b. complaining	
c. argumentativeness	
4. Confirming messages	
a. recognition	
b. acknowledgement	
c. endorsement	
B. How Communication Climates Develop	

1.   Escalatory conflict spirals
2.   De-escalatory conflict spirals

II.   **DEFENSIVENESS: CAUSES AND REMEDIES**
    A.   **Face-Threatening Acts**
    B.   **Preventing Defensiveness in Others**
       1.   Evaluation versus description
       2.   Control versus problem orientation
       3.   Strategy versus spontaneity
       4.   Neutrality versus empathy
       5.   Superiority versus equality
       6.   Certainty versus provisionalism

III.   **SAVING FACE: THE ASSERTIVE MESSAGE FORMAT**
    A.   **Behavior**
    B.   **Interpretation**
       1.   Based on experience, assumptions
       2.   Subjective
    C.   **Feeling**
    D.   **Consequence**
       1.   What happens to you, the speaker
       2.   What happens to the person you're addressing
       3.   What happens to others
    E.   **Intention**
       1.   Where you stand on an issue
       2.   Requests of others
       3.   How you plan to act in the future
    F.   **Using the Assertive Message Format**
       1.   Order may vary

2. Use personal style
3. Combine elements
4. Take your time

G. **Responding Nondefensively to Criticism**

　　1. Seek more information

　　2. Ask for specifics

　　3. Guess about specifics

　　4. Paraphrase the speaker's ideas

　　5. Ask what the critic wants

　　6. Ask about the consequences

　　7. Ask if anything else is wrong

B. **Agree with the Critic**

　　1. Agree with the facts

　　2. Agree with the critic's perception

　　3. Agreeing versus apologizing

KEY TERMS

aggressiveness

ambiguous response

argumentativeness

assertive message format

certainty

communication climate

complaining

confirming communication

consequence statement

constructive criticism

controlling communication

de-escalatory conflict spiral

defensiveness

description

disagreeing messages

disconfirming communication

empathy

equality

escalatory conflict spiral

evaluation

face-threatening act

feeling statement

Gibb categories

impersonal response

impervious response

incongruous response

intention statement

interpretation statement

interrupting response

irrelevant response

neutrality

problem orientation

provisionalism

sandwich method

spiral

spontaneity

strategy

superiority

tangential response

ACTIVITIES

10.1 UNDERSTANDING DEFENSIVE RESPONSES

LEARNING OBJECTIVES

- Identify confirming, disagreeing, and disconfirming messages and patterns in your own important relationships, and describe their consequences.

- Describe how the messages you identified in the previous objective either threaten or honor the self (face) of the communicators involved.

- Use Gibb's categories and the assertive message format to create messages that are likely to build supportive rather than defensive communication climates.

- Use the guidelines in this chapter to present critical messages in a constructive manner.

- Create appropriate nondefensive responses to real or hypothetical criticisms.

INSTRUCTIONS

1. Identify the person or people who would be most likely to deliver each of the following critical messages to you. If you are unlikely to hear one or more of the following messages, substitute a defensiveness-arousing topic of your own.
2. For each situation, describe
   a. the person likely to deliver the message.
   b. the typical content of the message.
   c. the general type of response(s) you make: attacking, distorting, or avoiding.
   d. your typical verbal response(s).
   e. your typical nonverbal response(s).
   f. the part of your presenting self being defended.
   g. the probable consequences of these response(s).

EXAMPLE

A negative comment about your use of time.
Person likely to deliver this message: *my parents*
Typical content of the message: *wasting my time watching TV instead of studying*
General type(s) of response: *attacking, distorting*
Your typical verbal response(s): *"Get off my back! I work hard! I need time to relax." "I'll study later;*
I've got plenty of time."
Your typical nonverbal response(s): *harsh tone of voice, sullen silence for an hour or two*
Part of presenting self being defended: *good student, not lazy*
Probable consequences of your response(s): *uncomfortable silence, more criticism from parents in the future*

1. Negative comment about your managing money.

   Person likely to deliver this message _____

   Typical content of the message _____

   _____

   General type(s) of response _____

   Your typical verbal response(s) _____

   _____

   Your typical nonverbal response(s) _____

   _____

   Part(s) of presenting self being defended _____

   Probable consequences of your response(s) _____

   _____

   _____

2. Criticism about your choice of friends.

   Person likely to deliver this message _____

   Typical content of the message _____

   _____

   General type(s) of response _____

   Your typical verbal response(s) _____

   _____

   Your typical nonverbal response(s) _____

   _____

Part(s) of presenting self being defended _____

Probable consequences of your response(s) _____

_____

_____

3. Criticism of a job you've just completed.

Person likely to deliver this message _____

Typical content of the message _____

_____

General type(s) of response _____

Your typical verbal response(s) _____

_____

Your typical nonverbal response(s) _____

_____

Part(s) of presenting self being defended _____

Probable consequences of your response(s) _____

_____

_____

4. Criticism of your schoolwork.

Person likely to deliver this message _____

Typical content of the message _____

_____

General type(s) of response _____

Your typical verbal response(s) _____

232

Your typical nonverbal response(s) _____

_____

Part(s) of presenting self being defended _____

Probable consequences of your response(s) _____

_____

_____

5. Criticism of your politics, political action, or lack of political involvement.

   Person likely to deliver this message _____

   Typical content of the message _____

   _____

   General type(s) of response _____

   Your typical verbal response(s) _____

   _____

   Your typical nonverbal response(s) _____

   _____

   Part(s) of presenting self being defended _____

   Probable consequences of your response(s) _____

   _____

   _____

6. A negative comment about your exercise (or lack of it).

   Person likely to deliver this message _____

233

Typical content of the message _____

_____

General type(s) of response _____

Your typical verbal response(s) _____

_____

Your typical nonverbal response(s) _____

_____

Part(s) of presenting self being defended _____

Probable consequences of your response(s) _____

_____

_____

234

10.2 DEFENSIVE AND SUPPORTIVE LANGUAGE

LEARNING OBJECTIVES

- Use Gibb's categories and the assertive message format to create messages that are likely to build supportive rather than defensive communication climates.
- Use the guidelines in the text to present critical messages in a constructive manner.
- Create appropriate nondefensive responses to real or hypothetical criticisms.

INSTRUCTIONS

1. For each of the situations below, write one statement likely to arouse defensiveness and one statement likely to promote a support climate.
2. Label the Gibb category of language that each statement represents (evaluation, description, control, problem-orientation, strategy, spontaneity, neutrality, empathy, superiority, equality, certainty, or provisionalism).

EXAMPLE

A neighbor's late-night stereo music playing is disrupting your sleep.

Defense-arousing statement: *Why don't you show a little consideration and turn that damn thing down? If I hear any more noise I'm going to call the police!*

Type(s) of defensive language: *evaluation, control*

Supportive statement: *When I hear your stereo music late at night I can't sleep, which leaves me more*

and more tired. I'd like to figure out some way you can listen and I can sleep.

Type(s) of supportive language: *description, problem orientation*

1. You're an adult child who moves back in with your parents. They say they expect you to follow the "rules of the house."

   Defense-arousing statement _____

   _____

   Type(s) of defensive language _____

   Supportive statement _____

   _____

   Type(s) of supportive language _____

2. Your roommate tells you you're trying to be "somebody you're not."

   Defense-arousing statement _____

   _____

   Type(s) of defensive language _____

   Supportive statement _____

   _____

   Type(s) of supportive language _____

3. A friend asks you what you see in your new romantic partner.

   Defense-arousing statement _____

   _____

   Type(s) of defensive language _____

   Supportive statement _____

   _____

   Type(s) of supportive language _____

4. Your boss says, "You call that finished?"

   Defense-arousing statement _____

   _____

   Type(s) of defensive language _____

   Supportive statement _____

   _____

   Type(s) of supportive language _____

236

5. Your friend buys the same thing you did after you bragged about the deal you got.

Defense-arousing statement _____

_____

Type(s) of defensive language _____

Supportive statement _____

_____

Type(s) of supportive language _____

6. On many occasions a friend drops by your place without calling first. Since you often have other plans, this behavior puts you in an uncomfortable position.

Defense-arousing statement _____

_____

Type(s) of defensive language _____

Supportive statement _____

_____

Type(s) of supportive language _____

7. Your roommate says, "You left the lights on *again*."

Defense-arousing statement _____

_____

Type(s) of defensive language _____

Supportive statement _____

_____

Type(s) of supportive language _____

8. Your parent praises your sibling for something without mentioning you.

   Defense-arousing statement _____

   _____

   Type(s) of defensive language _____

   Supportive statement _____

   _____

   Type(s) of supportive language _____

9. Your situation:_____

   Defense-arousing statement _____

   _____

   Type(s) of defensive language _____

   Supportive statement _____

   _____

   Type(s) of supportive language _____

238

10.3 WRITING ASSERTIVE MESSAGES

LEARNING OBJECTIVES

- Use the guidelines in the text to present critical messages in a constructive manner.

INSTRUCTIONS

Imagine a situation in which you might have said each of the statements below. Rewrite the messages in the assertive message format, being sure to include each of the five elements described in your text.

EXAMPLE

Unclear message: "It's awful when you can't trust a friend."

Assertive message :

Lena, when I gave you the keys to my house so you could borrow those clothes, I

came back and found the house unlocked. (behavior)

I figured you'd know to lock up again when you left. (interpretation)

I was worried and scared. (feeling)

I thought there was a break-in and was nervous about going in. (consequence)

I want to know if you left the house unlocked and, let you know how upset I am. (intention)

1. "Just get off my case; you're not my warden."

   _____ (behavior)

   _____ (interpretation)

   _____ (feeling)

   _____ (consequence)

   _____ (intention)

2. "I wish you'd pay more attention to me."

   _____ (behavior)

   _____ (interpretation)

   _____ (feeling)

_____ (consequence)

_____ (intention)

3. "You've sure been thoughtful lately."

_____ (behavior)

_____ (interpretation)

_____ (feeling)

_____ (consequence)

_____ (intention)

4. "You're the greatest!"

_____ (behavior)

_____ (interpretation)

_____ (feeling)

_____ (consequence)

_____ (intention)

5. "Matt, you're such a slob!"

_____ (behavior)

_____ (interpretation)

_____ (feeling)

_____ (consequence)

_____ (intention)

6. "Let's just forget it; forget I ever asked for a favor."

_____ (behavior)

_____ (interpretation)

10.4 MEDIATED MESSAGES – CLIMATE

LEARNING OBJECTIVES

- Identify confirming, disagreeing, and disconfirming messages and patterns in your own important relationships, and describe their consequences.
- Describe how the messages you identified in the previous objective either threaten or honor the self (face) of the communicators involved.

INSTRUCTIONS

Discuss each of the questions below in your group. Prepare written answers for your instructor, or be prepared to contribute to a large group discussion, comparing your experiences with those of others in your class.

1. Describe how the use of mediated forms of communication channels (e.g., telephone, e-mail) contributes to the communication climate (emotional tone) of your relationships.

   _____

   _____

2. Compile a list of the ways we can use mediated messages to recognize, acknowledge, and endorse others.

   _____

   _____

3. Give examples of how mediated messages have contributed to or helped minimize defensive spirals (negative, ineffective patterns of communication) in your relationships.

   _____

   _____

   _____

4. Your text describes ways we can respond nondefensively to criticism. In which mediated contexts can this skill be used most effectively?

   _____

   _____

10.5 CLIMATE ANALYSIS

LEARNING OBJECTIVES

- Identify confirming, disagreeing, and disconfirming messages and patterns in your own important relationships, and describe their consequences.

INSTRUCTIONS

Use the case below and the discussion questions that follow to discuss the variety of communication issues involved in effective communication. Make notes on this page, add other pages on your own, or prepare a group report/analysis based on your discussion. Add your own experiences to individualize the analysis.

Case

Gil and Lydia are brother and sister. They love one another and feel close. Their mother often tells Gil how wonderful Lydia is to call her so often, how smart Lydia is, what a good athlete she is, and how much she enjoys Lydia bringing home her friends to visit. Mom tells Lydia how generous Gil is, how hard he works, how many interesting things he does, and how well he manages money. The overall climate of the relationship between Gil and Lydia and their mother is good, but both Gil and Lydia find themselves getting defensive when their mom spends so much time praising the other.

1. Use aspects of Gibb's theory to explain why Gil and Lydia get defensive about these positive statements about the other.

   _____

   _____

   _____

   _____

2. Discuss situations similar to the one above in which people get defensive about statements that, on the surface, are positive and supportive.

   _____

   _____

   _____

   _____

244

3. Write coping with criticism responses for Gil or Lydia to use the next time their mother praises their sibling.

_____

_____

_____

4. How could Gil and Lydia's mother change the comments she makes about each sibling to reduce defensive reactions?

_____

_____

_____

10.6 APPLYING THE "SANDWICH METHOD"

LEARNING OBJECTIVES

- Use Gibb's categories and the assertive message format to create messages that are likely to build supportive rather than defensive communication climates.
- Use the guidelines in the text to present critical messages in a constructive manner.
- Create appropriate nondefensive responses to real or hypothetical criticisms.

INSTRUCTIONS

Read the first three scenarios below and apply the "sandwich method" to turn a possible defensive situation into a nondefensive one. Then describe two situations where you can apply the sandwich method in your own life and describe how you will apply this method.

1. You are working on a project for one of your classes with a partner. While your partner is friendly and contributes good ideas to the project, she always arrives late to your project meetings and spends the first 30 minutes of your work time talking about her new boyfriend. You wish the two of you could get to work sooner so you could complete the project and have more free time. Use the sandwich method to offer constructive criticism to your partner.

Positive Comment:

_____

_____

Concern:

_____

_____

Positive Comment:

_____

_____

2. Your new college roommate constantly returns to your dorm late at night and makes a lot of noise when saying good night to her friends. This noise wakes you up at night and you start to struggle to get up for your 7:30 am class. Use the sandwich method to offer constructive criticism to your roommate.

Positive Comment:

_____

_____

Concern:

_____

_____

Positive Comment:

_____

_____

3. One of your co-workers has a tendency to tell inappropriate jokes that you find offensive. Use the sandwich method to offer your co-worker some constructive criticism.

Positive Comment:

_____

_____

Concern:

_____

_____

Positive Comment:

_____

_____

247

Now apply the sandwich method to a situation in your own life.

Situation 1 Description_____

Positive Comment:

_____

_____

Concern:

_____

_____

Positive Comment:

_____

_____

Situation 2 Description_____

Positive Comment:

_____

_____

Concern:

_____

_____

Positive Comment:

_____

STUDY GUIDE

CHECK YOUR UNDERSTANDING

TRUE/FALSE

Mark the statements below as true or false. Correct false statements on the lines below to create true statements.

_____ 1. The tone or climate of a relationship is shaped by the degree to which the people believe themselves to be valued by one another.

_____ 2. Between confirming and disconfirming communication lie disagreeing messages.

_____ 3. Most experts agree that it is psychologically healthier to have someone ignore you than disagree with you.

_____ 4. Both positive and negative communication spirals have their limits; they rarely go on indefinitely.

_____ 5. In a marriage ignoring or "stone walling" a partner is a strong predictor of divorce.

_____ 6. Communicators strive to resolve inconsistencies or conflicting pieces of information because this "dissonant" condition is uncomfortable.

_____ 7. Using Jack Gibb's supportive behaviors will eliminate defensiveness in your receivers.

_____ 8. Constructive criticism can increase odds of successful confrontation, and rarely requires future acknowledgement.

_____ 9. The assertive message format works for a variety of messages: hopes, problems, complaints, and appreciations.

249

_____ 10. When you truly understand hostile comments, you just naturally accept them.

_____ 11. Verbal aggressiveness is the tendency to support the concepts of others and to relieve psychological pain of another.

_____ 12. Failure to return an e-mail is one example of lack of recognition.

COMPLETION

The Gibb categories of defensive and supportive behavior are six sets of contrasting styles of verbal and nonverbal behavior. Each set describes a communication style that is likely to arouse defensiveness and a contrasting style that is likely to prevent or reduce it. Fill in the blanks with the Gibb behavior described chosen from the list below.

evaluation	description	control	problem orientation	strategy
spontaneity	neutrality	empathy	superiority	equality
certainty	provisionalism			

1. _____ is the attitude behind messages that dogmatically imply that the speaker's position is correct and that the other person's ideas are not worth considering.

2. _____ is communication behavior involving messages that describe the speaker's position without evaluating others.

3. _____ is a supportive style of communication in which the communicators focus on working together to solve their problems instead of trying to impose their own solutions on one another.

4. _____ is a defense-arousing style of communication in which the sender tries to manipulate or deceive a receiver.

5. _____ is a supportive style of communication in which the sender expresses a willingness to consider the other person's position.

6. _____ is a defense-arousing style of communication in which the sender states or implies that the receiver is not worthy of respect.

7. _____ is a supportive communication behavior in which the sender expresses a message openly and honestly without any attempt to manipulate the receiver.

8. _____ is a defense-arousing behavior in which the sender expresses indifference toward a receiver.

9. _____ is a defense-arousing message in which the sender tries to impose some sort of outcome on the receiver.

10. _____ is a type of supportive communication that suggests that the sender regards the receiver as worthy of respect.

11. _____ is a defense-arousing message in which the sender passes some type of judgment on the receiver.

12. _____ is a type of supportive communication in which the sender accepts the other's feelings as valid and avoids sounding indifferent.

MULTIPLE CHOICE

Choose the letter of the defensive or supportive category that is best illustrated by each of the situations below.

a. evaluation
b. control
c. strategy
d. neutrality
e. superiority
f. certainty

g. description
h. problem orientation
i. spontaneity
j. empathy
k. equality
l. provisionalism

_____ 1. Gerry insists he has all the facts and needs to hear no more information.

_____ 2. Richard has a strong opinion but will listen to another position.

_____ 3. Lina kept looking at the clock as she was listening to Nan, so Nan thought Lina didn't consider her comments as very important.

_____ 4. "I know Janice doesn't agree with me," Mary said, "but she knows how strongly I feel about this, and I think she understands my position."

_____ 5. "Even though my professor has a Ph.D.," Rosa pointed out, "she doesn't act like she's the only one who knows something; she is really interested in me as a person."

_____ 6. "When I found out that Bob had tricked me into thinking his proposal was my idea so I'd support it, I was really angry."

_____ 7. "Even though we *all* wait tables here, Evanne thinks she's better than any of us—just look at the way she prances around!"

_____ 8. Clara sincerely and honestly told Georgia about her reservations concerning Georgia's planned party.

_____ 9. The co-workers attempted to find a solution to the scheduling issue that would satisfy both of their needs.

_____ 10. "It seems as though my father's favorite phrase is `I know what's best for you' and that really gripes me."

_____ 11. "You drink too much."

_____ 12. "I was embarrassed when you slurred your speech in front of my boss."

_____ 13. "The flowers and presents are just an attempt to get me to go to bed with him."

_____ 14. "She looked down her nose at me when I told her I didn't exercise regularly."

_____ 15. "Well, if you need more money and I need more help around here, what could we do to make us both happy?"

Choose the letter of the type of coping with criticism that is best illustrated by each of the situations below.

a. ask for specific details of criticism
b. guess about specific details
c. paraphrase to clarify criticism
d. ask what the critic wants
e. ask what else is wrong
f. agree with true facts
g. agree with critic's right to perceive differently
h. ask about the consequences

Criticism: "You never seem to care about much."

_____ 16. "Are you referring to my not going to the office party?"

_____ 17. "You're right that I didn't call you back within 24 hours."

_____ 18. "What do you want me to care more about?"

_____ 19. "I can see why you'd be upset with me for not coming to the party because you've told me you want me to be more involved with your work's social events."

_____ 20. "When I didn't come to the party, were you embarrassed or something?"

_____ 21. "So not calling you back right away was a problem. Have I upset you any other way?"

_____ 22. "So you're upset that I'm not visiting you every week, and you think that shows a lack of affection on my part—is that it?"

_____ 23. "What do you mean?"

_____ 24. "You're correct in that I couldn't visit this week because of finals."

_____ 25. "Because I wasn't at the party, it reflected badly on you."

252

Identify which element of an assertive message is being used in each statement according to the following key:

a. behavioral description
b. interpretation
c. feeling
d. consequence
e. intention

_____ 26. That's a good idea.

_____ 27. I'm worried about this course.

_____ 28. Jim looked angry today.

_____ 29. I want to talk to you about the $20 you borrowed.

_____ 30. I notice that you haven't been smiling much lately.

_____ 31. I don't know whether you're serious or not.

_____ 32. I'm glad you invited me.

_____ 33. Ever since then I've found myself avoiding you.

_____ 34. I'm sorry you didn't like my work.

_____ 35. I want you to know how important this is to me.

_____ 36. It looks to me like you meant to embarrass me.

_____ 37. After the party at Art's, you seemed to withdraw.

_____ 38. I see you're wearing my ring again.

_____ 39. From now on you can count on me.

_____ 40. I've never heard you say a curse word before.

_____ 41. . . . and since then I've been sleeping at my dad's house.

_____ 42. Because that occurred, they won't work overtime.

_____ 43. Dave sighed and looked out the window.

_____ 44. I'm excited about the possibility.

_____ 45. I'll get another place to live.

STUDY GUIDE ANSWERS

TRUE/FALSE

1.	T	3.	F	5.	T	7.	F	9.	T	11. F
2.	T	4.	T	6.	T	8.	F	10.	F	12. T

COMPLETION

1. certainty
2. description
3. problem orientation
4. strategy

5. provisionalism
6. superiority
7. spontaneity
8. neutrality

9. control
10. equality
11. evaluation
12. empathy

MULTIPLE CHOICE

1.	f	10.	b	19.	g	28.	b	37.	b
2.	l	11.	a	20.	b	29.	e	38.	a
3.	d	12.	g	21.	e	30.	a	39.	e
4.	j	13.	c	22.	c	31.	b	40.	a
5.	k	14.	e	23.	a	32.	c	41.	d
6.	c	15.	h	24.	f	33.	d	42.	d
7.	e	16.	b	25.	b	34.	c	43.	a
8.	I	17.	f	26.	b	35.	e	44.	c
9.	h	18.	d	27.	c	36.	b	45.	e

CHAPTER ELEVEN

Managing Interpersonal Conflicts

OUTLINE

Use this outline to take notes as you read the chapter in the text and/or as your instructor lectures in class.

I. THE NATURE OF CONFLICT
   A. Conflict Defined
      1. Expressed struggle
      2. Perceived incompatible goals
      3. Perceived scarce resources
      4. Interdependence
      5. Interference from the other
         party
   B. Conflict Is Natural
   C. Conflict Can Be Beneficial

II. CONFLICT STYLES
   A. Avoiding (Lose-Lose)
   B. Accommodating (Lose-Win)
   C. Competing (Win-Lose May
      Degenerate to Lose-Lose)
      1. Direct aggression
      2. Passive aggression
   D. Compromising (Partial Lose-Lose)
   E. Collaborating (Win-Win)
   F. Which Style to Use?
      1. Relationship
      2. Situation

255

2. Other person
3. Your goals

III. **CONFLICT IN RELATIONAL SYSTEMS**
   A. **Complementary, Symmetrical, and Parallel Styles**
     1. Complementary
     2. Symmetrical
     3. Parallel
   B. **Destructive Conflict Patterns: The Four Horsemen**
     1. Criticism
     2. Defensiveness
     3. Contempt
     4. Stonewalling
   C. **Conflict Rituals**
     1. Patterns of behavior
     2. Problematic if the *only* pattern

IV. **VARIABLES IN CONFLICT STYLES**
   A. **Gender**
     1. Socialization
     2. Situation
   B. **Culture**
     1. Individualism versus collectivism
     2. Low-context versus high-context
     3. Indirect and direct
     4. Ethnic background
     5. Personal choice

V. **CONSTRUCTIVE CONFLICT SKILLS**
   A. **Collaborative Problem Solving**
     1. Identify your unmet needs

2. Make a date

3. Describe your problem and needs
   a. clear messages
   b. listening and paraphrasing

4. Consider your partner's point of view

5. Negotiate a solution
   a. identify and define the conflict
   b. generate a number of possible solutions
   c. evaluate the alternative solutions
   d. decide on the best solution

6. Follow up the solution

B. Constructive Conflict: Questions and Answers

1. Isn't Win–Win too good to be true?

2. Isn't Win–Win too elaborate?

3. Isn't Win–Win negotiating too rational?

4. Is it possible to change others?

KEY TERMS

accommodating
avoiding
collaborating
competing
complementary conflict style
compromising
conflict

conflict ritual
crazymaking
direct aggression
parallel conflict style
passive aggression
relational conflict style
symmetrical conflict style

ACTIVITIES

11.1 UNDERSTANDING CONFLICT STYLES

LEARNING OBJECTIVES

- Identify the relational conflict styles, patterns of behavior, and conflict rituals that define a given relationship.

INSTRUCTIONS

1. For each of the conflicts described below, write responses illustrating the five types of conflict styles.
2. Describe the probable consequences of each style.

---

1. Your dad wants and expects you to spend every Thanksgiving with his whole extended family. You and some close friends who don't have large families want to get away for those four days and do something different. Your dad already arranged your transportation home.

Avoiding (lose-lose) response _____

_____

Probable consequences _____

_____

Accommodating (lose-win) response _____

_____

Probable consequences _____

_____

Competing response _____

_____

Probable consequences _____

_____

Compromising (partial lose-lose) _____

Probable consequences _____

Collaborating (win-win)_____

Probable consequences _____

2. A fan behind you at a ballgame toots a loud air horn every time the home team makes any progress. The noise is spoiling your enjoyment of the game.

Avoiding (lose-lose) response _____

Probable consequences _____

Accommodating (lose-win) response _____

Probable consequences _____

Competing response _____

Probable consequences _____

Compromising (partial lose-lose) _____

Probable consequences _____

_____

Collaborating (win-win)_____

_____

Probable consequences _____

_____

3. Earlier in the day you asked your roommate to stop by the store and pick up snacks for a party you are both hosting this evening. Your roommate arrives home without the food.

Avoiding (lose-lose) response _____

_____

Probable consequences _____

_____

Accommodating (lose-win) response _____

_____

Probable consequences _____

_____

Competing response _____

_____

Probable consequences _____

_____

Compromising (partial lose-lose) _____

_____

Probable consequences _____

_____

Collaborating (win-win)_____

_____

Probable consequences _____

_____

4. You and Marc share a cubicle and a computer at work and you are both responsible
    for the same amount and type of work. Marc arrives a few minutes earlier than you
    and stays on the computer for several hours, then begins his non-computer work.
    You would be able to work more efficiently if you had some time on the computer
    early in the day.

Avoiding (lose-lose) response _____

_____

Probable consequences _____

_____

Accommodating (lose-win) response _____

_____

Probable consequences _____

_____

Competing response _____

_____

Probable consequences _____

_____

261

Compromising (partial lose-lose) _____

_____

Probable consequences _____

_____

Collaborating (win-win)_____

_____

Probable consequences _____

_____

5. You and your spouse have to make a decision about your 5-year olds' schooling. You believe strongly in supporting public schools and having children attend the neighborhood school. Your husband believes he didn't get a good education in public school and since you can afford to, you should send your child to private school.

Avoiding (lose-lose) response _____

_____

Probable consequences _____

_____

Accommodating (lose-win) response _____

_____

Probable consequences _____

_____

Competing response _____

_____

Probable consequences _____

_____

Compromising (partial lose-lose) _____

_____

Probable consequences _____

_____

Collaborating (win-win)_____

_____

Probable consequences _____

_____

_____

What styles are easiest to use with family? With friends? At work? With strangers? Why?

_____

_____

_____

11.2 YOUR CONFLICT STYLES

LEARNING OBJECTIVES

- Identify the conflicts in your important relationships and how satisfied you are with the way they have been handled.
- Describe your personal conflict styles, evaluate their effectiveness, and suggest alternatives as appropriate.

INSTRUCTIONS

1. Use the following form to record three conflicts that occur in your life that you are comfortable analyzing.
2. For each, describe your behavior, show how it fits the definition of conflict, classify your conflict style, and describe the consequences of your behaviors.
3. Summarize your findings in the space provided.

INCIDENT	YOUR BEHAVIOR	HOW IT MEETS THE DEFINITION OF CONFLICT Expressed struggle Perceived compatible goals Perceived scarce resources Interdependence Interference of other party	YOUR CONFLICT STYLE Avoid Accommodate Compete Compromise Collaborate	CONSEQUENCES
EXAMPLE *My friend accused me of being too negative about the possibility of finding rewarding, well-paying work.*	*I became defensive and angrily denied his claim. In turn I accused him of being too critical.*	*This was clearly an expressed struggle and I perceived interference in my choice of jobs. Possibly we both perceived scarcity of the reward of feeling good about ourselves.*	*Competing*	*After arguing for some time, we left each other, both feeling upset. I'm sure we'll both feel awkward around each other for a while.*
1.				
2.				
3.				

CONCLUSIONS

1. Are there any individuals or issues that repeatedly arouse conflicts?

_____

_____

2. What conflict style(s) do you most commonly use? Do you use different styles with different people or in different situations? Why or why not?

_____

_____

_____

_____

3. You can go online to
http://jeffcoweb.jeffco.k12.co.us/high/wotc/confli1.htm and take a brief quiz about your approaches to conflict (are you a turtle, shark, bear, fox, or owl?). How do these animals compare to the labels used in the text?

_____

_____

_____

_____

4. Choose one or more of the conflicts you described in which you did not use a collaborative style and explain how you could have used a collaborative style. Predict what would have happened.

_____

_____

_____

_____

5. Are you satisfied with your usual way(s) of approaching conflict? Why or why not?

_____

_____

11.3 THE END VS. THE MEANS

LEARNING OBJECTIVES

- Identify the conflicts in your important relationships and how satisfied you are with the way they have been handled.
- Describe your personal conflict styles, evaluate their effectiveness, and suggest alternatives as appropriate.
- To distinguish the ends from the means in a personal conflict.

INSTRUCTIONS

1. In each of the conflict situations on the next page, identify the <u>ends</u> each party seems to be seeking. There may be ends that the relationship shares as well as individual ends for each of the parties involved. Ends in a conflict are the overall, general (often relational) goals that the dyad has.
2. Brainstorm a series of possible <u>means</u> that could achieve each person's (and the relationship's) ends. Means are the many possible ways to reach the end state.
3. Record conflict situations of your own, identifying ends and means.

CONFLICT SITUATION	SHARED ENDS	SPEAKER'S ENDS	OTHER'S ENDS	POSSIBLE MEANS
EXAMPLE *My friend wants me to visit her in Washington and meet her family. I'd like to visit, but it would cost a lot, and I'd rather save the money for something else.*	*We both want to maintain the affection in the relationship. We both want one another to know we are important to one another and that we care about one another and our families.*	*I want to spend as little money as possible while still letting my friend know how important she is to me. I don't want to lose her friendship.*	*She wants to show her family what a good friend I am and have some companionship while she has to stay in Washington.*	*She/her family sends me money to go to Washington. We share the cost. I combine whatever else I want to do with a short trip to Washington. We arrange for the family to meet me when they next come to our city. My friend comes back with her sister or mother to spend time with me.*

CONFLICT SITUATION	SHARED ENDS	SPEAKER'S ENDS	OTHER'S ENDS	POSSIBLE MEANS
1. My roommate wants a friend (whom I dislike) to sublease a room in our apartment.				
2. I'm dating a person who's of a different race than I am, and my family thinks this is a mistake.				
3. My older sister thinks that I'll turn into an alcoholic when I have a few beers (there are a few alcohol problems in our family). I tell her not to worry, but she won't get off my case.				
4. My mom keeps asking me about my grades and nagging me on the issue of my boyfriend. She thinks I'm going to make the same mistakes as she did.				

CONFLICT SITUATION	SHARED ENDS	SPEAKER'S ENDS	OTHER'S ENDS	POSSIBLE MEANS
5. Some people in my office listen to country music all day. I've got nothing against it, but it gets old. I'd like more variety.				
6. Your example:				

11.4 WIN–WIN PROBLEM SOLVING

LEARNING OBJECTIVES

- Identify the relational conflict styles, patterns of behavior, and conflict rituals that define a given relationship.
- Demonstrate how you could use the win-win approach in a given conflict.

INSTRUCTIONS

1. Follow the instructions below as a guide to dealing with an interpersonal conflict facing you now.
2. After completing the win-win steps, record your conclusions in the space provided.

Step 1: Identify your unmet needs (i.e., the situation, the person(s) involved, the history, etc.).

_____

_____

Step 2: Make a date. (Choose a time and place that will make it easiest for both parties to work constructively on the issue.)

_____

Step 3: Describe your problem and needs (behavior, interpretation, feeling, consequence, intention). Avoid proposing specific means or solutions at this point.

_____

_____

Step 3A: Ask your partner to show that s/he understands you (paraphrase or perception-check).

_____

_____

Step 3B: Solicit your partner's point of view/clear message (behavior, interpretation, feeling, consequence, intention).

_____

_____

_____

_____

Step 4: Clarify your partner's point of view (paraphrase or perception-check as necessary).

_____

_____

Step 5: Negotiate a solution.
   a. Restate the needs of both parties (what both have in common).

      _____

      _____

   b. Work together to generate a number of possible solutions that might satisfy these needs. Don't criticize any suggestions here!

      _____

      _____

      _____

      _____

      _____

   c. Evaluate the solutions you just listed, considering the advantages and problems of each. If you think of any new solutions, record them above.

      _____

      _____

      _____

   d. Decide on the best solution, listing it here.

      _____

272

Step 6: Follow up the solution. Set a trial period, and then plan to meet with your partner and see if your agreement is satisfying both your needs. If not, return to step 3 and use this procedure to refine your solution.

_____

_____

CONCLUSIONS

In what ways is this procedure similar to or different from the way in which you usually deal with interpersonal conflicts?

_____

_____

_____

Was the outcome of your problem-solving session different from what it might have been if you had communicated in your usual style? How?

_____

_____

_____

In what ways can you use the no-lose methods in your interpersonal conflicts? With whom? On what issues? What kinds of behavior will be especially important?

_____

_____

_____

What concerns or hesitations do you have about using the win-win approach? Why?

_____

_____

_____

11.5 MEDIATED MESSAGES – CONFLICT MANAGEMENT

LEARNING OBJECTIVES

- Identify the conflicts in your important relationships and how satisfied you are with the way they have been handled.
- To manage conflict in mediated contexts.

INSTRUCTIONS

Discuss each of the questions below in your group. Prepare written answers for your instructor, or be prepared to contribute to a large group discussion, comparing your experiences with those of others in your class.

1. In your experience, does conflict occur more rapidly or less rapidly in mediated contexts (e.g., e-mail, instant messaging/chat, telephone).

_____

_____

_____

2. Describe how mediated communication channels might help or hinder the brainstorming process (an important aspect of win-win problem-solving). Would the level of emotion involved make a difference? Why or why not?

_____

_____

_____

3. Describe gender and/or cultural differences in conflict management that might occur in mediated contexts.

_____

_____

_____

4. Describe whether in your experience certain mediated contexts tend to promote the use of particular conflict styles and whether or not conflict is easier or harder to manage using particular mediated channels.

_____

_____

_____

11.6 CONFLICT MANAGEMENT

LEARNING OBJECTIVES

- Identify the relational conflict styles, patterns of behavior, and conflict rituals that define a given relationship.

INSTRUCTIONS

Use the case below and the discussion questions that follow to discuss the variety of communication issues involved in effective communication. Make notes on this page, add other pages on your own, or prepare a group report/analysis based on your discussion. Add your own experiences to individualize the analysis.

CASE

Klaus and Drew have been roommates for two years, and they have had very few problems. But this term Klaus has a difficult and early class schedule, and he has taken on more hours at work to make ends meet. Drew's parents support him completely and he has a very light schedule this term. Klaus and Drew's friends continue to come to their house to party, and Drew is very irritated with Klaus because he's always studying and is a big bore all of a sudden. Klaus thinks Drew is a spoiled brat and insensitive to his needs. Neither Klaus nor Drew has said anything at this point.

1. Should Klaus and Drew bring this conflict out in the open? Would airing their differences be beneficial or harmful to the relationship?

_____

_____

2. What are the unmet needs of Klaus and Drew in this situation? Should they keep those unmet needs to themselves and use an avoidance style or should they use one of the other personal conflict styles?

_____

_____

_____

3. Evaluate the potential of the win-win problem-solving method to solve this situation.

_____

_____

11.7 ASSESSING YOUR CONFLICT STYLE

LEARNING OBJECTIVES

- Identify the conflicts in your important relationships and how satisfied you are with the way they have been handled.
- Describe your personal conflict styles, evaluate their effectiveness, and suggest alternatives as appropriate.

INSTRUCTIONS

Describe three conflicts that you have been in that did not have a successful resolution for you. Identify your conflict style in each and then describe what you could have done differently in this conflict.

Conflict 1 Description:

_____

_____

_____

Conflict Style_____

What you would have done differently?

_____

_____

_____

Conflict 2 Description:

_____

_____

_____

Conflict Style_____

What you would have done differently?

_____

_____

_____

Conflict 3 Description:

_____

_____

_____

Conflict Style_____

What you would have done differently?

_____

_____

_____

11.8 REPAIRING RELATIONSHIPS AFTER CONFLICT

LEARNING OBJECTIVES

- Describe the possible strategies for repairing a given relational transgression.
- Identify the content and relational dimensions of communication in a given transaction.

INSTRUCTIONS

1. Consider the various situations listed below.
2. Identify the type of transgression for each set of categories (columns two and three) and give your reasons for classifying it as you do.
3. Evaluate the options for repair along with the reasons you'd make the choice you do.
4. Record and analyze relational situations after conflict from your experience, your observations, films, or books.

SITUATION	TYPE OF TRANSGRESSION	IMPACT OF TRANSGRESSION	STRATEGIES FOR REPAIR
1. Your sibling works for the same company you do. You were applying for a promotion and really wanted the job. Unknown to you, your sibling also applied and got the job.			

SITUATION	TYPE OF TRANSGRESSION	IMPACT OF TRANSGRESSION	STRATEGIES FOR REPAIR
2. You and your (friend/partner/roommate—you choose) make plans to travel to Mexico together next summer. Each of you agrees to ask for the same weeks of vacation and sign up for the same flights. You request your time off, pay for your flights, and mentally prepare for the trip. Five weeks before the trip, the other person tells you he/she has decided not to "waste" a week of vacation in Mexico.			

STUDY GUIDE

CHECK YOUR UNDERSTANDING

TRUE/FALSE

Mark the statements below as true or false. Correct statements that are false on the lines below to create a true statement.

_____ 1. Gender and culture rarely have an impact on the types and styles of conflict.

_____ 2. Partners of self-silencers experience more frustration and discomfort when dealing with the avoiding partner.

_____ 3. It is best to adopt the attitude of curiosity when encountering a conflict with someone from another culture.

_____ 4. Effective communication during conflicts can actually keep good relationships strong.

_____ 5. Conflicts can never be constructive.

_____ 6. Passive aggressive styles can be seen as a type of competing.

_____ 7. Competing is clearly superior to other conflict styles to get what you want.

_____ 8. Crazymaking is just another name for passive aggression.

_____ 9. "It takes two to tango"—in conflict, as in dancing, men and women behave in totally similar ways.

_____ 10. The first step in win-win problem solving is to make a follow-up plan.

COMPLETION

Fill in the blanks with the crazymaker term described below.

avoiders   pseudoaccommodators   guiltmakers   subject changers   distracters
mind readers   trivial tyranizers   gunnysackers   beltliners   trappers

1. _____ don't respond immediately when they get angry. Instead, they let conflicts build up until they all pour out at once.

2. _____ do things they know will irritate their conflict partner rather than honestly sharing their resentments.

3. _____ engage in character analyses, explaining what the other person *really* means, instead of allowing their partners to express feelings honestly.

4. _____ set up a desired behavior for their partners and then when the behavior is met, they attack the very thing they requested.

5. _____ refuse to fight by leaving, falling asleep, or pretending to be busy.

6. _____ try to make their partners feel responsible for causing their pain even though they won't come right out and say what they feel or want.

7. _____ refuse to face up to a conflict either by giving in or by pretending that there's nothing at all wrong.

8. _____ use intimate knowledge of their partners to get them "where it hurts."

9. _____ attack other parts of their partner's life rather than express their feelings about the object of their dissatisfaction.

10. _____ escape facing up to aggression by shifting the conversation whenever it approaches an area of conflict.

MULTIPLE CHOICE

Match the terms below with their definitions.

_____ 1. win-lose

_____ 2. indirect communication

_____ 3. "Vesuvius"

_____ 4. conflict style

_____ 5. passive aggression

a. an indirect expression of aggression, delivered in a way that allows the sender to maintain a façade of kindness
b. an oblique way of expressing wants or needs in order to save face for the recipient
c. an uncontrolled, spontaneous explosion involved in conflict
d. an approach to conflict resolution in which one party reaches its goal at the expense of the other
e. a pattern of managing disagreements that repeats itself over time in a relationship

Choose the letter of the personal conflict style that is best illustrated by the behavior found below.

a. avoidance
b. accommodation
c. compete/direct aggression
d. compete/passive aggression
e. compromise
f. collaborate/win-win

_____ 6. Stan keeps joking around to keep us from talking about commitment.

_____ 7. "I can't believe you were so stupid as to have deleted the report."

_____ 8. Even though he wanted to go to the party, Allen stayed home with Sara rather than hear her complain.

_____ 9. Alternating bicycling and using a car, roommates are able to share expenses for only one car.

_____ 10. A smoker and nonsmoker agree that smoking on the balcony meets both their needs.

_____ 11. Rather than tell Nick about his frustration over Nick's not meeting the deadline, Howard complained to others about Nick's unreliability while maintaining a smiling front to Nick.

_____ 12. Carol wouldn't answer the phone after their disagreement because she was afraid it would be Nancy on the other end.

_____ 13. Seeing John's obvious distress, Terrell put aside his work to listen to John for a half-hour. This didn't totally meet either's needs, but did partially meet each person's needs.

_____ 14. Even though Sage could see Kham's distress, she told him she had a deadline to meet in one hour and asked if they could talk then.

_____ 15. (Sarcastically) "Oh, sure, I *loved* having dinner with your parents instead of going to the party Saturday night."

Choose the best answer for each statement below.

16. When partners use different but mutually reinforcing behaviors, they illustrate a

    a. complementary conflict style.
    b. symmetrical conflict style.
    c. parallel conflict style.
    d. supportive conflict style.

17. Research suggests that partners of "self-silencers" (people who avoid conflict) often feel
    a. relieved that they never fight.
    b. encouraged to be more honest.
    c. frustrated and uncomfortable.
    d. none of the above

18. Partners who fight but are unsuccessful at satisfying important content and relational goals have a _____ style.

    a. intimate-aggressive
    b. intimate-nonaggressive
    c. nonintimate-nonaggressive
    d. nonintimate-aggressive

19. Partners who avoid conflicts—and one another—instead of facing issues head-on have a(n) _____ style.

    a. intimate-aggressive
    b. intimate-nonaggressive
    c. nonintimate-nonaggressive
    d. nonintimate-aggressive

20. Partners who have a low amount of attacking or blaming, who confront one another either directly or indirectly, but manage to prevent issues from interfering with their relationship have a _____ style.

    a. intimate-aggressive
    b. intimate-nonaggressive
    c. nonintimate-nonaggressive
    d. nonintimate-aggressive

CHAPTER 11 STUDY GUIDE ANSWERS

TRUE/FALSE

1. F	3. T	5. F	7. F	9. F
2. T	4. T	6. T	8. T	10. F

COMPLETION

1. gunnysackers	5. avoiders	9. distractors
2. trivial tyranizers	6. guiltmakers	10. subject changers
3. mind readers	7. pseudoaccomodators	
4. trappers	8. beltliners	

MULTIPLE CHOICE

1. d	5. a	9. f	13. e	17. c
2. b	6. a	10. f	14. f	18. d
3. c	7. d	11. d	15. c	19. c
4. e	8. b	12. a	16. a	20. b